MANAGING
ACTIVITIES & RESOURCES

**SECOND
EDITION**

ROGER BENNETT

KOGAN
PAGE

First published in 1989 by
Kogan Page Ltd, in association with
the National Extension College,
18 Brooklands Avenue, Cambridge CB2 2HN, and
the Institute of Supervisory Management,
22 Bore Street, Lichfield, Staffordshire WS13 6LP.
This edition published in 1994 by Kogan Page Ltd.

Kogan Page Limited
120 Pentonville Road
London N1 9JN

British Library Cataloguing in Publication Data
A CIP record for this book is available
from the British Library.

ISBN 0 7494 1267 4

Typeset by Photoprint, Torquay, South Devon
Printed in England by Clays Ltd, St Ives plc

Contents

Extracts from the Preface to the First Edition

The three books in this series are about practical management skills, particularly those interpersonal supervisory skills which enable managers to communicate effectively, influence others, lead, plan, coordinate and control. More than ever before, business requires managers who are formally trained and competent in practical administrative technique: in skills that are anchored against *occupationally relevant* competencies immediately applicable in any sort of organisation, and not against abstract theories and applications suited mainly to the needs of very large firms. The books attempt to combine theory with practice and to provide the reader with a working knowledge of current legislation relevant to the supervisory management field, of management concepts and the latest techniques.

Together the three books comprise a skills building programme designed to springboard a newly appointed or junior manager — concerned primarily with supervisory and executive management — to a level of competence at which he or she can assume a more responsible role. After reading these books you should be able to undertake a variety of useful practical management tasks: counsel, make a presentation, chair a meeting, write a job description, negotiate, appraise the performances of employees, and so on.

I gratefully acknowledge the permission granted by the editors of *Modern Management*, the *Training Officer* and *Export* for the use of materials previously published in these journals in article form. Parts of Chapters 2 and 3 are based on material prepared for my Pitman text *Organisation and*

Management. I thank Pitman Publishing for their kind permission to adapt this material. Thanks are also due to the Equal Opportunities Commission for permission to reproduce parts of its Code of Practice on the avoidance of discrimination in employment.

Preface to the Second Edition

These new editions of the three books in the *Effective Supervisory Management* series contain fresh material on a number of recently introduced EC Directives; empowerment; the use of visual aids when making presentations; government guidelines concerning the treatment of employees with HIV; flexible working methods and just-in-time procedures; total quality management; and the 1993 Health and Safety at Work Regulations. Legal references plus the sections on maternity pay and SSP have been revised and updated.

I am indebted to Rosalind Bailey for word-processing the amendments to the manuscript, and to Kogan Page Ltd for their efficient processing of the texts.

Roger Bennett

The Effective Supervisory Management Series

The Effective Supervisory Management Series provides a step-by-step guide to every aspect of the modern supervisory manager's role. Comprising three books, all of which have been completely revised and up-dated in their second editions, the series gives comprehensive coverage of the following syllabuses:

- **National Examining Board for Supervisory Management (NEBSM) — formerly NEBSS — Supervisory Management Certificate**
- **The Institute of Supervisory Management (ISM) Certificate in Supervisory Management Studies**
- **The Institute of Bankers (IOB) Banking Certificate – "Supervisory Skills" and Diploma — "Nature of Management".**

Specially designed for use by supervisors at all levels of responsibility, these three books can be used individually or as a reference pack to be consulted time and time again. Each chapter commences with a set of objectives which, by the end of the chapter, the reader will have achieved. Focusing on state-of-the-art management methods, particularly those involving information technology and the crucially important Codes of Practice which affect managerial issues, each chapter then concludes with a succinct summary of the key points.

The three books in the series are:

Managing People
Managing Activities and Resources
Personal Effectiveness

1

The Business Environment

Objectives

At the end of this chapter you will be able to:

- distinguish between the various forms of business units in the UK
- identify the basic activities of the firm
- identify the objectives of your organisation and be aware of the constraints that exist.

Organisations operate within commercial, economic, legal and political environments that substantially determine their structures and conduct. Businesses are organisations formed to provide the products and services that consumers demand. Various types of business organisation exist and businesses need not be privately owned: the state may provide goods and services instead of commercial firms. British industry is composed mainly of sole trader businesses, partnerships and limited companies.

Types of business

Sole traders

A sole trader is an independent self-employed person who owns and personally controls a business, assuming full responsibility for its activities and debts. Sole traders carry all the risks of business failure and are liable for outstanding debts even to the extent of their personal wealth. They have a direct interest in their businesses, overheads can be kept to a minimum, and there is instant decision taking. The financial affairs of a sole trader are private except in relation to tax. However, sole traders often experience difficulties in raising finance for expansion, and economies of scale cannot normally be obtained.

Partnerships

Partners in a business will (usually) each contribute capital and participate in managing its affairs. All partners are jointly liable for the debts of the firm and the partnership as a whole is bound by all contracts entered into by any partner provided the contracts relate to the business. In the absence of a written agreement partnerships are governed by the Partnerships Act 1890, which states (among other things) that:

- all partners shall share equally in managing and in the profits of the partnership
- new partners may not be admitted without the consent of all existing partners
- disputes shall be settled by simple majority vote, unless the dispute concerns the fundamental nature of the partnership's work in which case a unanimous vote is necessary
- the partnership automatically ends on the death, insanity or personal bankruptcy of a partner, or if a partner is convicted of a criminal offence.

Self-check

To what extent are sole traders and partners personally liable for the debts of the business?

Answer
In both cases the concept of unlimited liability applies. In other words, the personal wealth of the owner/s may be used to settle any outstanding business debts, as, in the eyes of the law, the business and the owner/s are one.

In the case of partnerships, each partner is jointly and severally liable, which means that, should your fellow partners have no personal assets, you may be held liable for the whole debt to the extent of your personal assets.

The Act allows for 'sleeping partners' who contribute capital but leave the running of the business to other partners. A sleeping partner may obtain protection against personal liability for the debts of the business by registering the fact that he or she is only a sleeping partner (unable to write cheques or enter contracts on behalf of the business) with the Registrar of Companies at Companies House.

Partnership is a common and popular mode of business organisation. Through pooling skills and resources, larger and more versatile businesses may be formed, although policy disagreements between partners often arise and decision taking can thus be slow and inefficient.

Limited companies

A limited liability company has its own legal personality. It enters into contracts in its own name and can sue and be sued as an identity entirely independent of its owners. Shareholders (owners) of a limited company are responsible for its debts only to the extent of their shareholdings. There are three types of limited company: private, public, and limited by guarantee.

Private limited companies cannot invite the general public to subscribe to their shares or debentures. The overwhelming majority of limited companies are private, existing primarily to avoid the owners being personally responsible for company debts. Many private companies have a nominal share capital of £100, of which only a small part is actually called up. Public companies may raise capital from the general public. They are not obliged to do so but in practice the vast majority of public companies do in fact invite the public to subscribe.

All registered companies must prepare audited final accounts and a balance sheet and deposit these with the Registrar at Companies House. Public companies need at least two shareholders and a minimum of £50,000 of share capital, of which one quarter must be paid up on each share. They must have at least two directors and a company secretary (who might also be a director). Private companies require a minimum of two shareholders, one director and a secretary. Companies limited by guarantee are limited companies without share capital where the members guarantee that if the company ceases to trade and cannot pay its debts then they will each make a small contribution (say £1) towards the outstanding balance. Such companies are widely used for educational and other non-profit making institutions which, nevertheless, engage in trade and thus require limited liability.

Activities within the business firm

Businesses undertake four basic activities: finance, marketing, operations and personnel. Operations might involve production — in which case manufacturing techniques, product design, research and development, raw materials procurement and quality management will figure prominently in the firm's priorities — or they might concern the provision of a service, such as banking, consultancy or serving customers in a shop.

Research and development are important for manufacturing firms. Research concerns the acquisition of new technical knowledge, particularly regarding new products, processes, materials and working methods. Activities might be initiated by the marketing department (having identified new consumer demands) or by the production department as it seeks new methods of manufacture. Development on the other hand means the practical application of the results of research. Often, development activities require adaptation of the discoveries of other firms. In fact, much work described as research is really development, and few organisations distinguish between the two functions. Whether the greatest benefits accrue to 'pure' (ie exploratory and theoretical) research or to applied, immediately relevant and practical research is open to question. Applied research offers quick returns, and may itself provide the impetus for major theoretical developments. Yet truly original and creative thinking might not be possible through applied research. Whichever its form, research itself may be organised 'functionally', so that each researcher specialises heavily in a narrow area of research, or via project teams within which all aspects of a research problem are considered and openly discussed. In choosing an appropriate organisational structure for conducting research, much depends on the extent of specialised equipment and knowledge required and how much co-ordination of activities is needed to expedite the project.

Marketing

Marketing is more than selling, though (obviously) higher sales is always the ultimate aim. Rather, marketing is a whole collection of activities including advertising, selling and sales-promotion, marketing research, introduction of new products, pricing, packaging, distribution and after sales service. Marketing research is not the same as market research. The latter concerns investigations into the sizes and structures of markets in terms of age, sex, income, occupation etc of consumers whereas marketing research includes enquiries into other aspects of marketing as well. Examples of marketing research are studies into the effectiveness of advertising, packaging research, evaluation of sales methods and the analysis of consumer behaviour. The marketing concept is the idea that supply of goods and services should be a function of the demands for them. There is little point in producing goods which people are not prepared to buy. This statement is not as innocuous as it first appears; it implies that marketing and not production staff should decide finally what goods should be produced.

Activity

The writer has identified four basic activities common to all organisations: finance, marketing, operations and personnel.

Take a few minutes to consider the marketing section of your own organisation and make a list of the functions it performs. As you read on, compare your list of functions with those mentioned in the next.

Marketing departments can be organised by function, product or region. A functional structure will arrange staff into sections corresponding to particular activities such as advertising, distribution, personal selling etc. Product organisation divides a department into groups which deal with all aspects of marketing specific products. An individual group will be responsible for advertising, selling and distributing just one product, it will not be concerned with other products. The advantage of product organisation is that staff develop several marketing skills and gain experience of a wide range of marketing problems, though the obvious benefits of narrow concentration in specialist areas (packaging or public relations for example) will not be obtained. Product organisation is common in small firms that cannot afford specialised functional departments. For large decentralised firms covering wide geographical areas, regional marketing organisation might be appropriate. One office could cover the north east of a country, another the north west. Within each region a product or functional form of organisation could then be imposed.

Application of the marketing concept in practice implies the integration of marketing with other business activities. The marketing manager must liaise closely with design and production staff, with accountants, transport managers, advertising agents and salespeople in the field. Also, marketing executives must be involved in corporate planning, sales forecasting, training of marketing personnel and the development of new products. Of course, conflicts between marketing and other departments can arise. Production staff, naturally, will want research expenditures to be devoted to innovation in manufacture and process development rather than to the innovation of entirely new products whose production feasibility is unclear. Accountants might be reluctant to authorise large expenditures on intangible advertising activities (message strategies or corporate identity projects for example) that have no resale value. Cost accountants sometimes favour product standardisation, whereas marketing staff typically insist on product variety and diversification to meet differing marketing demands. Adoption of the marketing concept will not guarantee cures for all a firm's ailments, but it does enable a firm to base its objectives on realistic assessments of customers' needs.

Price policy is crucially important in marketing. Note however that although price is a vital factor in the purchasing decision, it is not necessarily paramount. Much depends on consumers' perceptions of the unique attributes of a product: its quality, reliability, image and 'need fulfilling' characteristics. The price a firm can charge depends in part on total consumer demand for the product involved. This is determined by the number of consumers, their incomes, seasonal factors and expectations of future price changes. If demand is highly responsive to price alterations, so that a small reduction in price leads to a large increase in sales, a price cut will be economically worthwhile because extra sales will more than compensate for reduced unit revenue. Note, however, that other firms may match or undercut price reductions, engage in additional advertising or alter their designs. A small business that attempts to undercut larger rivals risks being put out of business by competitors who can use their superior resources to cut prices so low that the small firm cannot survive.

Production costs are of course a major factor affecting price. Firms must at least break even. But the volume of sales necessary to break even depends on the unit price (high prices enable low volume break-even points), while the number of units sold itself depends substantially on the unit price (high prices are normally associated with lower sales). Thus, firms must balance price and resulting sales against production costs. Unfortunately, unit production costs themselves depend on the volume of sales because of fixed overheads. For instance, a factory rent of £10,000 spread over 100 units gives an overhead cost of £100 per unit; yet if 200 units are produced the unit cost becomes £50 per item. In practice, a firm will usually predetermine the length of a production run, add up all its anticipated costs — fixed and variable — and divide estimated total cost by planned output. Some percentage mark-up is then added to get a unit price. The problem here is that firms typically produce several different products so that allocations of overheads to the various items are necessarily arbitrary. Consequently, individual products may be over- or under-priced.

Price policy influences many aspects of a firm's operations: wages paid to staff, production techniques, administrative expenses and so on. Also, the image that a business projects might depend critically on its price strategy — high prices can imply high quality. Clearly, then, great attention must be devoted to choosing a price. Several pricing strategies are available to the firm. With 'penetration pricing', for example, low prices are combined with aggressive advertising to gain larger shares of existing markets. The strategy is suitable where large outputs lead to reductions in unit costs through economies of scale, but will not succeed if competitors can reduce their prices to correspondingly low levels. Note that prices should not be set so low that they are not credible to consumers. There exist 'confidence levels' for prices below which consumers lose faith in a product's quality. Low prices can create in consumers' minds perceptions that goods are shoddy, incomplete, have inadequate guarantees or offer poor after sales service.

The term 'skimming' is used to describe a high price policy whereby a firm attempts to 'skim the cream' from the top end of a market by charging high prices for luxury versions of established products. High quality images are needed to justify the high prices charged. Successful skimming requires significant numbers of high income consumers prepared to pay top

Self-check

What is the distinction between fixed and variable costs?
Study the list of costs below, and categorise each as either fixed
or variable.

— rates
— wages of assembly line workers
— salaries of office staff
— telephone expenses
— materials used on an assembly line
— materials used in the office
— depreciation on equipment.

Answer
Variable costs change in conjuction with levels of output,
therefore, as output increases, so variable costs increase.

Fixed costs are incurred by a business irrespective of the level
of output and will only change over time. Therefore, even at
zero output, the business will have to pay these costs.

Fixed costs: depreciation; material in office; telephone;
                salaries; rates
Variable costs: materials on assembly line; wages of assembly
                workers

---

prices. If production costs are low the firm will earn exceptionally high profits. In consequence, other firms will be attracted
into operating at the top end of the market. The firm must
convince consumers that its high price version offers distinct
improvements over the standard model sold by competitors.
Products should be designed to appeal to affluent consumers,
offering extra features, greater comfort, versatility or ease of
operation.

'Target pricing' means that the firm predetermines a target
level of return, and fixes its prices at levels that will achieve this
for a given estimated volume of sales. With 'price discrimination', different prices are charged in different markets for the
same good. There must be barriers — geographical distances,
high transport costs, or consumer ignorance — that prevent
customers buying in one market and reselling at a profit
elsewhere. The practice of 'limit pricing' results from the fact
that high prices accompanied by high sales will result in big
profits that will attract competing firms. Thus, existing firms

may lower their prices to levels where new entry to the industry would not be worthwhile because of the startup costs the entrants would have to incur. Firms earn less in the short term than if they charged higher prices, but their long term security is assured. 'Variable pricing' means that a firm increases its prices when its order book is full, and reduces them as business slackens. This is not a common technique; customers resent having to pay different prices for the same product at different times.

Self-check

Distinguish between price discrimination, skimming and penetration pricing, as pricing policies.

Answer

Price discrimination: you charge different prices in different markets for the same product

Skimming: high prices are charged for luxury versions of established products

Penetration pricing: low prices are charged in order to achieve high levels of turnover.

Obviously, in determining pricing policy, the organisation will have to cover the cost of production, but the policy should also reflect the market you are aiming at and the image of the product itself.

Personnel

Many aspects of the personnel function are dealt with extensively in other chapters. Basically, personnel management concerns the recruitment, training, appraisal and dismissal of staff, and industrial relations between management and trade unions. Specific responsibilities include human resource planning (ie assessing future labour requirements and ensuring they will be met), job analysis, training, redundancy procedures and dealing with health and safety at work. Today, most medium to large firms employ a personnel officer, essentially because of increased governmental regulations relating to contracts of employment, dismissal procedures, health and safety etc and in recognition of the enormous importance of human relations in employment situations. In many firms, the role of the personnel manager is largely advisory, with line managers taking ultimate responsibility for personnel affairs. In this case, a personnel department would for example advertise a vacant post and prepare (with the help of the 'user' department in which the successful candidate will work) a shortlist of candidates, but the final decision on who to appoint will rest with line managers in the user department concerned. Further advice will be offered on staff grading, payment, promotion policies, grievance procedures and general employee relations.

Personnel officers experience many problems which stem from the generic nature of their work. Conflicts with other managers can arise about who exactly has authority over specific functions (line executives may regard personnel department's participation in decision making as unwarranted interference) and about the extent to which a personnel officer should represent employees' rather than management's interests. Sometimes a personnel officer will sympathise with employees' points of view, even though personnel work is strictly a management function. The personnel officer might be called on to implement disagreeable managerial policies.

Accounts

The accounts (or finance) department will prepare cash flow forecasts, budgets, cost analyses, financial accounts and other financial information for management control. Accounting systems monitor revenues and expenditures, and quickly establish the firm's financial position at particular times. Firms need to know the values of their fixed assets (land, buildings, vehicles, plant and equipment) and current assets (stocks, debtors, work in progress and cash in hand). Every transaction contributes to profits (or losses) and must therefore be recorded accurately and stored in an easily extractable form. Accounts should indicate areas of inefficiency, and reveal the exact costs of all the firm's activities. Accurate and detailed accounts will make policy formation easier and facilitate the well-organised implementation of corporate plans.

Major business financial accounts are the profit and loss account and the balance sheet. The former, as its name implies, shows income, expenditure, payments to shareholders and transfers to and from reserves during the period covered after allowing for unpaid overdue bills (creditors) and amounts

---

Activity

Does your organisation have a separate personnel section? If so, what functions does it perform? Is there any friction between personnel specialists and line managers?

The majority of organisations will have a separate personnel section, staffed by experts in that field. Functions will vary but may include recruitment, training, promotion, industrial relations, health and safety, staff appraisal and manpower planning.

Line managers want to have the major say in who should be recruited, promoted etc and friction is likely to occur where there is a difference of opinion.

---

owing to the business but not yet reclaimed. The balance sheet summarises a firm's financial situation at a particular date. It is divided into two parts: assets and liabilities. Assets are the possessions of the business (premises, stock, cash etc); liabilities show the people and institutions who own the assets or to whom they are owed. Liabilities include owner's capital, bank loans, tax payable, creditors and dividends due to shareholders.

The fundamental purpose of a balance sheet is to provide information: to management, shareholders, creditors, potential investors and the tax authorities. Interpretation of financial accounts is an important topic which is dealt with more fully in chapter 7 below. Note here, however, that the analysis of balance sheets is made difficult by ambiguities in asset and liability values resulting from (subjective) choice of depreciation method, revaluation criteria, stock valuation, decisions regarding when to regard money owing as bad debts, how much profit to retain, sizes of reserves and so on.

An important finance department function is to monitor the use of working capital within the firm. Working capital is current assets minus current liabilities. It represents the resources available to finance expansion of sales or production independent of fixed assets. It shows also the extent to which new fixed assets may be purchased from internal funds once current liabilities have been met. Working capital is money tied up within the business and should generally be kept to a minimum. Current assets comprise stocks, debtors and cash. Low average stockholding levels associated with high rates of turnover are desirable because money invested in stock is idle.

It should be earning profits instead. Current liabilities consist principally of creditors who, in effect, are helping in the short term to finance the firm.

Self-check

Study the following list and mark each item as either an asset or a liability.

— bank overdraft
— content of petty cash box
— debtors (those who owe you money)
— creditors (those to whom you owe money)
— stock of finished goods
— shareholders' funds
— debentures
— land
— motor vehicles.

Answer
Assets: petty cash, debtors, stock, land, motor vehicles
Liabilities: bank overdraft, creditors, shareholders' funds, debentures.

Fixed assets are for permanent use within the business. Premises are an obvious example. Additions to and deletions from fixed assets during the accounting period must be shown and assets are valued in net terms, having allowed for depreciation. Assets must be written off (depreciated) over their economic lives so that the true worth of the business is known. Depreciation is regarded as a source of funds because it reduces profits and thus retains money within the business. There are several techniques for depreciating assets, but two: 'straight-line' and 'diminishing-balance', are very common. Straight-line depreciation writes off an asset by the same amount each period, whereas the diminishing-balance approach deducts a predetermined percentage of the net value of the asset at the end of each year. Hence, assets are never completely written off. Depreciation by diminishing-balance writes off progressively lower amounts as time goes by and assets retain value for much longer periods. While some assets decrease in value, others (land for example) might appreciate over time. Revaluation of fixed assets at higher figures will create profits that go into the balance sheet as a separate item in the fixed assets category, under the title 'revaluation reserve'.

Another important item that sometimes appears in balance sheets as a fixed asset is the 'goodwill' of the firm. Goodwill is an intangible fixed asset. It arises when a business has been purchased for a price higher than the value of its assets. Goodwill represents the worth of the firm as a going concern — its good name, reputation, existing customers and suppliers, technical knowledge, trained personnel, the state of its order book — independent of its physical possessions. Other intangible fixed assets include ownership of patents, licences, trade marks, trading concessions and similar rights.

Consistency in valuation criteria, and continuous application of the same techniques, are necessary for meaningful interpretation of a company's accounts, since trends may then be isolated and, hopefully, causes of change identified. Difficulties arise in comparing the balance sheets of various firms. Contrasting valuation techniques might be used; economic environments differ. Nevertheless, inter-firm comparisons are frequently attempted, by investors seeking high yield shares and by individual managements for internal appraisal. Note that business conditions can quickly alter. Relationships between variables often change. Also, balance sheet figures show situations only on a particular date, they need not reflect normal operations. Indeed, an unscrupulous management might deliberately manipulate balance sheet magnitudes immediately before a financial year end in order to make its financial position appear favourable.

European Union influences

Britain's membership of the European Union (EU) has had enormous consequences for businesses, especially since the completion of the Single Market. Laws and practices that applied for centuries have been swept aside and replaced by fresh rules and standards. Company law has had to be altered to comply with EC directives, as have technical product standards, health and safety legislation, the law on intellectual property, agency law, public procurement arrangements, and the law on advertising, marketing, sales promotion, competition, mergers and aquisitions, and consumer protection. Also, despite British objections, a greatly expanded European Union role in labour relations and employment protection is seemingly assured.

Directives and regulations

EU decisions are implemented mainly through 'directives' and 'regulations'. A directive specifies a necessary outcome (eg to achieve equal pay for work of equal value carried out by men and women) but allows the government of each member country to introduce its own particular legislation to achieve the desired objective. Regulations are laws that apply immediately and equally throughout the Union: national governments have no discretion over the wording of the legislation. A 'draft directive' is one that has been put forward by the European Commission but has yet to be agreed by EU member countries.

Community directives and regulations now apply to a large number of business practices, including:

- the content and presentation of company accounts;
- the conduct of merger and takeover bids;
- implementation of mass redundancies by companies;
- avoidance of sex discrimination at work;
- the employment rights of pregnant women;
- work involving visual display units.

Additionally, there are many important draft directives concerning, *inter alia*, the participation of employee representatives in the management of large companies, the extent of the management information to be given to employees, rules on night working, and the rights of part time and casual employees.

The wider environment

Organisations exist within societies possessing unique political systems, cultures, laws, attitudes and beliefs. A business must obey the laws and conventions of the society of which it is a part. More than ever before, cultural and other environments are susceptible to rapid and far reaching change and organisations must learn how to respond quickly and effectively to fast changing environmental circumstances. Changes in transport, communications systems, electronics and information technology are particularly significant. Change in technical, economic and social environments is today inevitable. The problem is how best to adapt.

A country's culture affects citizen's perceptions of moral

worth and thus influences individual behaviour. Society regulates relationships within and between organisations, both formally through its legal system and informally through customs and norms. Consequently, societal factors affect industrial relations, industrial structures, relations between firms and their customers and suppliers and methods of doing work. And the attitudes created by social pressures help determine many economic variables (productivity, consumer demand, competitive conditions, the distribution of income and wealth) as well as the prevailing physical environment.

The political system defines the manner in which industry is organised — businesses are but elements of a wider politico-economic structure, so that changes in the structure must affect business organisations and their management. The interfaces between a business and its economic environment are numerous. Firms are taxpayers, suppliers of goods and services, buyers of raw materials and other factor services, employers of labour and providers and consumers of technology. They must balance conflicting demands from various interest groups: workers want higher wages, shareholders more dividends, consumers lower prices and so on. The political superstructure defines the legal environment of business, particularly in relation to the law of contract, health and safety at work and employment and consumer protection.

Marketing is perhaps the most important interface between the firm and society, since it brings the business directly into contact with the public. Pressure groups representing consumers' interests have complained about several aspects of the way some firms market their products — misleading advertisements, poor quality goods, built-in product obsolescence, inadequate after-sales service — and have demanded and obtained laws to protect consumer interests. Consumerists demand four basic rights: information, choice, safety and redress. Monopolistic power over markets, they suggest, reduces consumers' abilities to choose among products, while advertisements that focus on images rather than objective facts cause ignorance of products (especially products which can damage health) among potential consumers.

Such criticisms have led to demands for laws and regulations to protect the consumer, particularly the low income consumer and those who do not possess the technical competence to evaluate the claims of professional marketing personnel. Thus, critics argue, legislation is needed on such matters as weights and measures, competition, price control, labelling and advertising messages. In Britain, laws such as the Misrepresentation Act (preventing retailers making false statements about merchandise), the Sale of Goods Act 1979 — which requires sellers to sell goods of merchantable quality which are fit for their intended purposes — and the Trade Descriptions Acts 1968 and 1972 (outlawing false descriptions of goods), are in part the result of consumerist pressure.

Social responsibility of business

Most (though not all) businesses seek to maximise their profits. Do businesses have a moral obligation also to serve the public interests of the society of which they are a part? Many firms do in fact consciously seek to be good employers paying 'fair wages', enriching jobs, practising equal opportunity recruitment and promotion systems etc and good neighbours avoiding environmental pollution and actively participating in community affairs, but others do not and there are many laws (anti-price fixing laws, constraints on how debts may be collected, prohibition of insider trading in stocks and shares, after-sales guarantee and compulsory insurance requirements, and so on) to protect the public from business organisations. Additionally, numerous voluntary restraints (particularly government backed Codes of Practice) and other non-enforceable advisory regulations have emerged.

Activity

Organisations do not exist in a vacuum and are influenced by external factors, be they political, economic, social or technological.

Identify three external factors that have influenced your organisation during the past five years or so.

The external factors you have identified may have been beneficial or threatening to your organisation, but they will have influenced decision-making. Examples identified may range from UK government legislation, to the strength of the US$, to the price of oil to the latest developments in new technology.

Two major approaches to social responsibility issues exist. One view is that the unbridled pursuit of profit necessarily leads to a society that is just. According to this argument, profit maximising firms will always produce the goods that consumers most desire (as evidenced by the prices they are willing to pay) since otherwise maximum profits cannot be obtained. Concern for intangibles such as equal opportunities or the quality of the environment are treated by advocates of this approach in much the same way as demands for goods. If people want the environment to possess certain characteristics they will pay for those characteristics, and organisations will naturally spring up that (in return for payment) will seek to manipulate the environment to satisfy the public's desires. Social considerations, they argue, need not concern individual firms. Managers are not trained or competent in social work and should not interfere in social affairs.

The alternative view is that state intervention is essential for ensuring that firms do not behave in irresponsible and socially damaging ways. Large businesses possess enormous economic and, by implication, social power. They can manipulate communities and appropriate for themselves revenues far in excess of those justified by their contributions to the wider society. Firms are able to initiate social change, and it is reasonable therefore that society, through its elected representatives, determine the directions that changes should take. Successful businesses expand and eat up their less successful rivals, but eventually monopoly situations will exist that then enable firms to exploit consumers, and the decisions of big businesses necessarily affect local communities — shut down decisions cause unemployment, loss of incomes and social distress, wages policies affect community spending and so on.

Summary

This chapter has shown you that there are different types of business organisations in this country, but while the nature of the business may vary, there are many common elements. Now it is time to look more closely at your own organisation:

- what is the nature of its business and how is it structured
- what are its objectives
- how does it balance the profit motive with social obligations?

2
Organisation

Objectives

This chapter will help you to:

- explain approaches to organisation structure, in particular current thinking on the design of organisations
- select the most appropriate structure to meet the needs of your organisation
- organise your own department effectively.

Organisations are associations of people who come together to achieve particular goals. They are characterised by centres of leadership which guide them towards their objectives, conscious divisions of labour, authority and responsibility and internal systems of communication and control. To 'organise' work is to arrange its performance through rationally determined structures. Work is broken down into manageable units which are then allocated to various individuals and departments. Company organisation begins with strategic directives issued by the board of directors, who act on behalf of shareholders. The board delegates authority to senior managers in charge of specific functions: finance, marketing, personnel etc. Senior managers in turn delegate to middle managers, who then delegate to heads of department and other executives.

Organisation is the structural framework within which business activities occur and devising the system for allocating work to departments and choice of the personnel to whom tasks should be assigned is one of the most important duties management must perform. Patterns of authority, responsibility and accountability have to be fashioned and employees made aware of their duties. Individuals should know whose instructions they should obey and in what circumstances. Unfortunately, demarcations between departmental and personal responsibilities are sometimes confused, with subordinates receiving conflicting instructions from different superiors. There is need, therefore, for explicit division of authority within the firm. To meet this need, many firms issue formal statements that define precisely the roles of various employees. Typically (though not always) chains of command are illustrated in 'organisation charts' showing patterns of authority and control.

Organisation charts

The aim of an organisation chart is to clarify individual responsibilities and to define the system of accountability within the organisation. A simplified example of an organisation chart is shown in Figure 2.1.

Associated with each position in the diagram is a job specification stating the duties and responsibilities of that particular post. Horizontal as well as vertical linkages can be included to highlight areas of mutual concern and joint responsibility (though the resulting diagrams might be complicated and difficult to understand). A major benefit of preparing an organisation chart is that it forces management to specify the pattern of accountability within the firm. Also, new employees — who will be given a copy of the organisation chart on appointment — will be in no doubt about their roles and responsibilities.

A criticism of organisation charts is that they encourage inflexible approaches to spheres of responsibility, the scope of individual duties, interdepartmental relations and so on — structural inconsistencies not shown in an organisation chart lie behind many organisational problems. Charts illustrate nothing more than a *desired* organisational structure at a specific moment in time. They do not reveal emotional conflicts, personal favouritism, or differences in senior management's perceptions of the calibres of various employees. Only formal relationships are highlighted. On paper, a certain person might have just one superior, but in practice that individual might actually report to several different superiors depending on the particular aspect of the job. Business environments continually

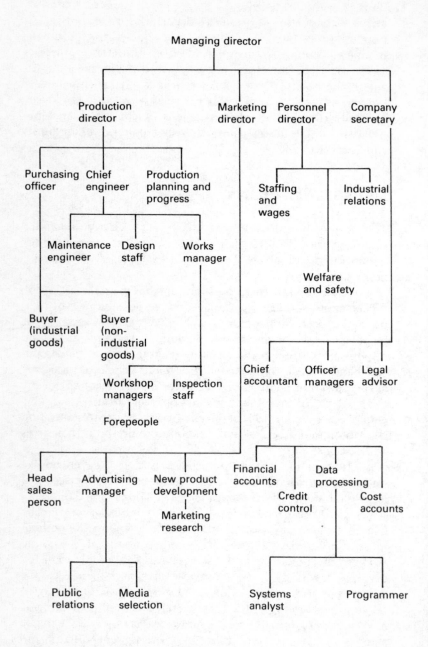

Figure 2.1   An organisation chart

change and organisations need to be able to respond quickly and effectively to new external situations.

Organisation charts can quickly become out of date and, if so, the effort spent on their preparation is wasted. Moreover, relationships within an organisation are typically far more complex than they appear in the diagram. Note also that actual behaviour is frequently influenced by *informal* channels of communications, indeed, informal channels can be faster and more efficient than the official system. Rigid adherence to bureaucratic formal procedures can inhibit initiative and effective decision taking.

Line and staff

Organisation charts are good for showing line and staff relationships within the firm. The line structure identifies points of contact between managers and their subordinates. Each position in the system shows the authority of its occupant and to whom that person is responsible. Vertical communications proceed only through the line system; if a manager cannot handle a problem it is referred upwards to superiors. Equally, work may only be delegated to the subordinates of a specific position.

The 'staff' organisation is advisory to the line system. It consists of specialists who give expert advice to line executives but who do not themselves take important decisions. Line managers ask staff advisers for assistance, yet are not obliged to accept their advice. Lawyers, researchers, industrial relations specialists and technical experts are likely to occupy 'staff' positions. Sometimes, staff managers are empowered to implement their own decisions within certain predetermined areas. For example, a personnel officer may be authorised to select media to carry job advertisements, but not to choose applicants for certain positions.

It is usual for either the line or the staff structure to dominate. Line dominated systems possess unambiguous chains of command and clearly defined areas of responsibility. They are coherent and easy to comprehend, but they relegate non-executive specialists to subsidiary roles. Moreover they rely heavily on a few key personnel. Resignation or sudden illness of an important line manager can cause an entire administrative system to collapse. Staff dominated structures enable line executives to avoid immersion in detailed analysis of technical issues, but tend to concentrate power into a few pairs of hands. The small number of line managers available to take executive decisions finds itself the centre of authority, receiving advice from an army of specialist counsellors. This type of organisation can succeed, provided line executives possess sufficient ability and stamina to cope with the heavy demands made upon them.

Compromise solutions are not uncommon, with staff managers possessing some degree of executive authority. This lifts the burden of routine decision making from line executives, but in so doing creates formidable problems of coordination and control. Relationships are complicated, and responsibilities may be unclear. Breakdowns in communications and, consequently, duplication of effort occur. However, there is no danger of staff specialists undermining the authority of those they advise (who may respect the expert knowledge of the staff adviser more than they respect the decision taking ability of an immediate line boss). Also staff specialists are made accountable for their actions.

Self-check

What is meant by the terms, line and staff relationships and functional organisation?

Answer

Line relationships indicate the points of contact between managers and subordinates. Line managers are given the power to take decisions. Staff relationships mean that any expert advice given to a line manager by a staff adviser need or need not be accepted. Functional organisation is an attempt to give those experts occupying 'staff' positions an opportunity to take and implement decisions within their field of expertise.

Finding an appropriate balance between line and staff modes of organisation can be difficult, especially in fast changing commercial environments. Ignoring staff specialists' expertise can be fatally expensive, notably where legal regulations or new production or marketing techniques are involved. Yet, ultimately, a strong line system is needed to get things done — staff specialists are sometimes infatuated with technical minutiae and devote too much time and resources to esoteric matters.

Such problems have caused managements to rethink fundamentally the usefulness of orthodox line and staff approaches to organisation, notably in high-tech industries where technical progress (requiring complete organisational restructuring) advances rapidly. One important result has been the emergence of 'matrix' organisation structures.

Matrix organisation

This began among firms operating within fast changing high-tech environments. It relates specific functional requirements to the skills available within the firm, creating 'project teams' across departmental boundaries. The idea is illustrated in the highly simplified example shown in Figure 2.2.

This shows how various sections of major departments contribute to particular functions — which may be defined as narrowly as the firm requires. We see that the credit control section has interests in the selling and distribution functions; that the personnel department representative reponsible for industrial relations should have a say in determining policy for (among other things) work study (efficiency) exercises and so on. Committees can now be assembled to oversee the administration of any area of the firm's business. Of course, a real matrix would be far more extensive and detailed than the above. It would name individual people within departments and identify their areas of activity. Sub-matrices can be drafted for departments and sections.

Matrix organisation offers a practical and coherent device for analysing the makeup of an enterprise. Personal and departmental contributions to the organisation are systematically classified and crucial activities that absorb large amounts of effort and resources are highlighted. The method is commonly used where several departments performing related duties are grouped together into divisions. In this way, interdepartmental communications are enhanced and duplication of effort avoided. Note that matrix structures do not show authority systems, which makes them especially suitable for joint activities that involve colleagues of equal rank. Each team will need a leader/facilitator responsible for publicising its aims, securing agreement on the tasks that must be completed and on policies and accountability and obtaining resources from external sources. Project work involves much coordination and planning leading therefore to many meetings and much committee work.

	FINANCE			PERSONNEL		
Function	*Costing section*	*Data processing*	*Credit control ... etc.*	*Recruitment section*	*Industrial relations*	*Wages and salaries ... etc*
MARKETING						
Sales			✓			✓
Distribution		✓	✓			
Packaging	✓					
New product development	✓					
(plus other marketing functions advertising, research, etc.)						
PRODUCTION						
Design	✓					
Labour deployment		✓		✓	✓	
Efficiency	✓			✓	✓	
Production control	✓					✓
Purchasing	✓	✓				
Stock control		✓				
etc						
PERSONNEL						
etc						

Figure 2.2 A matrix organisation

Matrix structures were first used in the US in the 1950s, notably in the aerospace industry where rapid technical advance and the pressing need to solve complex practical problems led to the abandonment of traditional management hierarchies. Orthodox distinctions between 'line' and 'staff' functions are so blurred in high technology environments that classical approaches to organisation — unity and chain of command, narrow span of control etc (see below) — become irrelevant. With matrix systems, each team is given its own budget and authority to implement decisions. Teams are multidisciplinary, cutting across traditional organisational and occupational boundaries.

Supervisors in matrix systems need to be flexible both in the duties they undertake and their involvement with other sections. Authority is shared and confusion about who precisely is responsible for which function may ensue. Project leaders are entirely responsible for their projects, though heads of department remain and have functional authority over their own departments. In consequence, team members might receive conflicting instructions from heads of department and project team leaders so it is important to establish at the outset who, ultimately, each individual should obey and whether subordinates are to regard themselves first and foremost as members of a department or as members of a particular project team. Usually, departments take precedence since projects last only for limited periods, and individuals will normally be assigned to a number of projects at the same time.

Self-check

How does the matrix structure differ from traditional line/staff structures?

Answer

Matrix is a more modern approach to structuring organisations and is an attempt to build more flexibility into the system. While recognising the need for functional expertise, it tries to build in team spirit and independence by bringing experts together to work on a specific project. The number in the team and the expertise required will be dictated by the nature of the assignment and all team members will report to the project leader, rather that individual functional heads of department.

Inevitably, there is duplication of effort in matrix systems. Against this, however, is the fact that matrix organisations offer exciting opportunities for the practical application of participatory approaches to management and the rapid development of decision taking skills. Junior staff are given scope to contribute to managerial work; there is interdepartmental cross-fertilisation of ideas and interdisciplinary transmission of managerial expertise. Also, separation and compartmentalisation of management functions is avoided: each element in the structure has to be dovetailed into the organisation as a whole and in so doing senior management is compelled to ensure that all the elements interlock. Management becomes, therefore, a coordinatory rather than directive activity. Further advantages include the following:

- the downgrading of rank and occupational status in decision taking processes can generate enthusiasm and innovation among junior staff, while employees' simultaneous involvement in several projects develops healthy attitudes to the acceptance of change. Membership of teams can be quickly altered to meet new and unexpected technical and other demands
- matrix schemes can support project based management by objectives programmes, with individual performances being appraised against their contributions to successful completion of particular projects
- junior staff gain first hand experience of management and decision taking within an environment of participation, joint activity and high motivation towards achieving collective goals.

Activity

Analyse the structure of your own organisation and identify any improvements that might be made.

Organisation structures tend to change very little over time. Those changes that do take place are usually re-groupings of staff, the underlying philosophy remains the same. No system is perfect, but attempts to change it are usually met with hostility.

The chapter will now go on to consider how to supervise a project team. If you have had any experience of this, spend a few minutes writing down your own ideas, then read on.

Supervising a project team

Your role as leader of a project team is to coordinate rather than direct, so you should aim to facilitate the generation of new ideas and create a climate in which members' natural enthusiasm will develop. Team members are sometimes unclear about the precise nature of their roles, especially if they have no experience of project work. They look for hierarchies within groups and might even create new and unnecessary status differentials where hierarchies do not already exist. With project based systems, however, responsibility for decision taking is shared, and fast and efficient project completion, not occupational rank, is the primary criterion for determining the allocation of work. Two problems can emerge: firstly, the development of charismatic leaders within teams who, although popular as individuals, are not as technically competent as other members and, secondly, the reluctance of some members to perform low status tasks. Yet, if all members are to contribute to important decision taking and the development of new ideas, they should all contribute to the completion of both innovative development and routine work. Imagine the paradoxical situation of having (say) a six person team designing a new ignition system for a motor car, meeting two or three times a week, pooling ideas, reporting on individual assignments, brain storming etc — but then assigning *all* mundane and boring duties (filing, petty correspondence, minor secretarial work) to just two or three members. Suppose moreover that the members performing low status tasks come up with the best innovative ideas. How then can high status members reconcile their avoidance of routine work (justified by superior occupational rank) while occupying secondary roles in important development matters? Resentments and interpersonal conflicts, fundamentally incompatible with the ethos and efficiency of a well run project team, will arise.

Decentralisation and divisional control

Decentralisation is an important feature of many large companies, indeed, all organisations are 'decentralised' to a greater or lesser extent. Note that decentralisation is not the same as delegation, since an organisation may be divided into regional, industrial, product or other divisions without any one division becoming subservient to the rest. Nevertheless, all decentralised structures require some central control and the issue is how much 'regional' autonomy the central control should allow. Much depends on the calibre of the personnel in charge of divisions, on the communications systems linking divisions to the centre and on the quality of information flows.

There is perhaps a natural tendency for large organisations to decentralise, since this allows 'local' control over operations thus enabling the centre to concentrate on long term strategic plans. Decentralisation may occur through the creation of subsidiary companies or through the divisionalisation of a single firm that retains a single corporate identity. In a tightly controlled organisation an inner administrative body takes all significant decisions, and issues *binding* directives to divisions (or subsidiaries).

Divisions

Divisional managers follow pre-determined roles and procedures, exercising little discretion in their work. Note that the larger the organisation the harder it becomes for top management to take all important decisions affecting divisions, so that some delegation of divisional authority has to occur.

The aims of divisionalisation are improved efficiency, less red tape, better divisional decision taking and faster response to environmental change. In a loosely controlled system, decisions are taken by local (though not necessarily geographically disparate) managers with expert knowledge of local conditions, within budgetary constraints imposed by the centre. Typically, divisional heads are given targets by the centre in the context of an overall corporate plan, but are then left to achieve objectives in their own ways. The advantages of divisionalisation include motivation of divisional managers who can use their own initiative in solving problems, its value in training local managers for more senior central posts and the relative ease with which divisional activities can be integrated by the central control. Disadvantages are the duplication of effort involved, losses of economies of scale and specialisation and the possibility of divisions regarding themselves as independent bodies with objectives different to those of the parent organisation. Rivalries between divisions may emerge, with divisions vying for attention and additional resources.

Self-check

Identify three benefits and three problems associated with decentralisation.

Answer

Benefits: less red tape, able to respond quickly to local needs, management able to use own initiative, motivates staff, good training ground for senior management

Problems: duplication of effort, loss of economies of scale, lack of standard practice, lack of rules to follow, lack of cooperation between divisions, rivalries, empire building

Do not worry if the points you identified are not included in the above, as it is not an exhaustive list.

Organisational design

There is no single organisational structure universally applicable to all situations. Choices are necessary, and organisations can be tailor made to suit particular circumstances. The sorts of decision to be taken include:

- whether to organise the firm around products, functions or people
- the widths of spans of control (see below)
- degrees of overlap between responsibilities
- the extent of specialisation and the division of labour
- how individual and departmental activities are to be controlled and co-ordinated.

Other factors relevant to organisational design are the nature of the firm's objectives and the external environment within which the business operates. As objectives change so too will the relevance of the firm's organisational structure. For instance, a business which operates in a fast moving, technically sophisticated industry may find that a competitor introduces a new product which renders all existing models obsolete. The firm must react instantly by altering its own product line. This can involve complete reorganisation of methods of production, marketing and administration. A flexible structure that can be quickly altered is most appropriate here. The nature of the external environment is a significant determinant of organisational choice. Examples of variables affecting wider commercial environments are the laws and/or customs of society, market structures, the degree of market uncertainty, local business practices, perhaps even the local political system. Changes in laws on employment protection, for example, or the publication of a new government Code of Practice might affect company personnel policies or an alteration in company law might require a complete restructuring of the financial makeup of the firm.

Also important for organisation design are employees' attitudes, morale, abilities and educational attainments; and the ease of communication within the company. Organisations which use highly qualified staff for specialist tasks may need to adjust their organisation structures to meet the emotional requirements of this type of worker. If information flows smoothly through the business and if interpersonal and inter-departmental relations are good, a relatively complicated organisation structure may be appropriate.

Span of control

A manager's 'span of control' is the number of immediate subordinates he or she controls. 'Wide' spans involve (say) 15 or 20 subordinates, narrow spans contain just two or three. Most authorities suggest that any more than six or seven subordinates represents too wide a span of control because of the complex relationships and competing demands on the controlling manager's time that result. Four factors are relevant to the choice of a span of control: organisational diversity, complexity of work and the calibres of the manager and his or her subordinates.

Organisational diversity affects the efficiency of internal communications. If face to face contacts between manager and subordinates are impossible, communication depends on telephone calls, letters, memoranda and similar indirect means. Interruptions in information flows and other communications breakdowns cause loss of effective control, especially if people and departments are geographically separated. Complex work means that managers need time to assess the reports and suggestions of subordinates and they ought not to be over-burdened with minor problems arising from lower levels. A narrow span of control is appropriate in this case.

Some managers are better able to handle large numbers of subordinates than others, depending on their training, experience and personal qualities. The degree of authority given to the manager is also relevant here. Similarly, well-trained, enthusiastic and competent subordinates need less control and supervision than others, so that wide spans of control may then be applied.

Self-check

What are the main factors that will influence span of control?

Answer

Span of control is the number of persons or activities controlled by an individual supervisor.

While there can be no hard and fast rule, you should be guided by:

— complexity of the work; the greater the complexity, the more narrow the span of control
— organisational diversity; the greater the geographical distance the more narrow the span of control
— calibre of subordinates; when dealing with well-motivated, well-trained, competent staff, a manager can cope with a wider span of control
— calibre of manager; some managers, due to experience, personality etc, are able to exercise effective control over larger numbers of staff.

Narrow spans of control recognise that an individual's capacity to supervise others is limited and that it is better to deal with a small number of subordinates properly than to have contact with many subordinates but only in casual ways. However, wide spans also offer advantages — they force managers to delegate (so that subordinates acquire experience of higher level work), subordinates may experience a higher degree of job satisfaction and the cost of supervision is low. On the other hand, coordination of subordinates' activities may be poor. Communication between subordinates of equal rank could be inadequate and lead to much duplication of effort.

Organisations possessing narrow spans of control are often characterised by 'bureaucracy'. There is much planning, clear division of work and many levels of authority. The word bureaucracy is used pejoratively in everyday language, but in

> **Activity**
>
> What do you understand by the term bureaucracy and what characteristics does a bureaucratic firm posses?
>
> It is highly likely that your concept of bureaucracy is one of rules, red tape and petty officials. While this is true to an extent, the bureaucratic approach can bring some benefits.
>
> As you read on, you will be introduced to Max Weber's view of bureaucracy. Compare the features mentioned in the text with those in your own list.

management studies it has a technical meaning as well. Bureaucracy — as an administrative concept — is concerned with the systematic regulation of activities via formal and impersonal rules and the establishment of clearly defined hierarchies. Max Weber, a sociologist, studied the bureaucratic mode of organisation in great detail and listed its distinguishing features.[1] According to Weber, bureaucracy is a *rational* institutional response to the organisational needs of industrial society, and exhibits the following characteristics:

- extensive and binding systems of rules with precedents, standardised procedures, and stable and continuous inter-departmental relations; rules and decisions are always recorded, in writing
- application of the managerial division of labour, specialisation of functions, precise definitions of authority and responsibility structures
- hierarchical patterns of administration with 'unity of command'
- separation of policy making from administration. Decisions are based on expert technical advice; control of staff is purely impersonal.

Bureaucracy, Weber noted, is the logical consequence of the divorce of business ownership (shareholders) from day to day executive control. The occupant of a particular office never actually *owns* any part of the system. There are distinct divisions between various grades of staff and established procedures for communicating between them (including well developed procedures for appeal against higher level decisions).

Executive management relies upon written rule books that are followed to the letter, thus relieving officials of the need to exercise judgement and interpret events. Managers are 'professionals', they are technically competent and pursue logically structured careers with regular promotions, training and staff development, and a pension on retirement.

Within a 'Weberian' bureaucracy, staff enjoy security of tenure, a social esteem directly linked to occupational status, fixed salaries, career development and protection from arbitrary dismissal. Weber regarded bureaucracy as the most efficient form of organisation. It was logical, self-perpetuating and could resist external pressures for change. The practice of following existing norms and precedents, without question, meant that administrators could avoid having to exercise discretion, since relatively few unique problems would arise. However, bureaucracies are threatened by the large volumes of 'red tape' they generate and the possibility that actual behaviour within the organisation might be influenced by charismatic leaders who are not part of the official hierarchy.

A further problem is that bureaucracy can stifle initiative. True — job descriptions are precise and objectively determined (so that if a particular person resigns or retires the job can go on) but this precision itself encourages personnel not to think or act independently. Individual creativity and originality is extinguished by the stringency of rigid legalistic frameworks. Bureaucracies are not good at accommodating change — they follow precedents and hence apply outdated solutions to problems and the ritualistic work routines imposed in bureaucratic systems cause the detailed minutiae of work to become an end in itself — ignoring its relevance to the achievement of the organisation's wider goals. There is much 'passing the buck' and resistance to new ideas, especially where multidisciplinary approaches are required. Slow decision taking might result from the existence of many levels in the hierarchy and much time may be wasted on pursuing irrelevant objectives.

The bureaucrat is never 'wrong'. He or she can defend every action by referring to the appropriate rule or procedure. Relationships are impersonal, and, because of their predictability, create trust among colleagues: an *esprit de corps* arises. Staff identify with the organisation, even if they occupy relatively lowly positions, although frustrations can emerge among junior staff if the chain of command is exceptionally long. Often, junior staff in bureaucracies have no means of immediate access to those who take decisions; resulting perhaps in unthinking conformity to the status quo.

Self-check

Identify two advantages and two disadvantages of bureaucracy.

Answer
Points mentioned might include:
Advantages: logical, able to resist external pressure for change, rule book to follow, standardised pattern of behaviour
Disadvantages: stifle initiative, red tape, reluctance to take decisions, cannot accommodate change.

Departmentation

The first and possibly most important decision in designing the organisation of a business (or other) enterprise concerns the structuring of departments. A 'department' is a set of activities under a particular manager's control. Departments may be defined in product, function, market or personal terms.

Product departmentation means creating departments, each of which deals with a single product or service. Department staff control all activities associated with the good, including purchase of raw materials, administration of processing and the sale and distribution of the final product. Senior departmental managers acquire a wide range of general managerial skills. They become experts in the problems associated with their own product. This specialised knowledge might be essential if the firm produces technically complicated goods. An advantage of product departmentation is that coordination between relevant functions and stages of production is easily achieved. Performance appraisal is relatively straightforward in product department systems, since profit and cost centres are easily defined. Managers' performances can be measured against the costs, revenues and output levels of a product.

Market departmentation occurs when departments are constructed around geographical regions or particular customer types (regional sales offices, or a separate department to deal with wholesale customers, for example). It may be cheaper to locate a department near to customers; local factors may then be taken into account when deciding policy. Similarly, market departmentation could relate to customer size (eg special facilities for large buyers), or to various distribution channels, export or home markets etc. Problems of coordination may ensue, and some loss of central control will be experienced. As with product departmentation, this method necessarily involves the duplication of activities. To avoid this, many organisations establish departments to cover specific functional areas — production, accounts, transport, administration and so on. The major functional departments contain sections, so that an advertising department, for example, might be sub-divided into sections for media selection, sales promotions, package design and other promotional activities. The responsibilities of functional departments follow logically and naturally from the work of the organisation and will parallel occupational distinctions. Everyone concerned with selling will be in the marketing department, all who are involved in manufacture will be in production and so on. Functional departmentation is easy to understand but may encourage narrow and introspective attitudes. Departments with wider responsibilities might provide staff with challenging environments that stimulate effort and initiative. Another problem here is that functional specialists, production managers for instance, often develop patterns of thought and behaviour related more to their specialisms than to the well-being of the organisation as a

---

Self-check

Distinguish between product departmentation and market departmentation.

Answer

There are many different approaches to structuring an organisation, and one firm might adopt different approaches in different areas.

Product departmentation means that you group all staff activities together based on product or service. In this way, all functional staff become experts associated with their product or service.

Market departmentation groups people together within geographical area or customer type. One department would be selling the complete range of products or services to people within their geographical area or customer group.

whole. It is essential therefore that staff within a single functional department be regularly exposed to, and preferably involved with, the work of other departments. Matrix organisations (see above) are helpful in this respect.

In small family businesses it is common for departments to be created around specific people. As new functional needs arise they are allocated according to the interests of the family members. Eventually, each department controls a variety of unrelated activities. A partner in a small firm might for example be interested in finance and advertising. Thus, all things concerned with these functions will be dealt with in that partner's department.

Organising your department

Employees need to know what exactly is expected of them and how their activities fit into the work of the firm. List your department's objectives and describe briefly the activities necessary to achieve them. Make a note of all the constraints that might prevent the successful completion of these activities, and how they might be overcome. Ask yourself how much sectional specialisation is possible, and whether specialisation will improve or worsen subordinates' morale. If specialisation is appropriate, examine how you can best integrate the efforts of various subordinates towards the achievement of common departmental goals. How will you ensure that the right job is done at the right time and in the right way? Is extra training needed to enable staff to work effectively within your intended organisational framework?

In structuring the tasks that your subordinates perform you are in fact structuring the content of their working days, so ensure that certain people are not left with insufferably repetitious and boring workloads. Divide work evenly and fairly, ensuring that everyone has at least some non-routine and challenging duties to perform. Next, draft outline job specifications for each position and include in each description a statement of the aims of the job. Check that jobs do not overlap and are congruent with departmental aims. Now draft an organisation chart (or matrix) and assess whether each position within the structure possesses sufficient authority and resources for effective operation. Look for possible coordination problems, conflicts of interest and potential clashes of personality among subordinates. Determine spans of control, who shall be responsible to whom and tell the people involved about the proposed structure, inviting their comments.

Once established, the authority structure will determine the departmental chain of command — instructions can only be given to an *immediate* subordinate. It is unwise for a senior person to bypass a level of authority when issuing orders, since the staff to whom instructions are given might then receive conflicting orders from their immediate superiors, who themselves may bitterly resent their authority being (as they see it) undermined.

Aim always to *clarify* personal roles, objectives and relations with other positions and be realistic about your expectations of the volume of work that each subordinate can reasonably be expected to perform.

The next thing to consider is how easily subordinates can communicate laterally in order to solve problems without having to refer them to a higher level. Specify the types of problem you expect people to sort out themselves and those you expect to be passed upwards, and tell each subordinate who they should consult for advice on various issues.

Analyse the intended workflow, determining the stages through which each work unit must pass and the levels of authority at which decisions relating to it must be taken. Identify points of contact with other departments for various jobs. Each work unit begins as someone's input and ends as an output from that person, so make sure that outputs and inputs coincide as work changes hands. Examine the implications of the proposed workflow for the layout of the department and analyse its role in the work of the firm as a whole. Does it, for example, supply work to a single recipient, or to several? Is the department capable of completing all its formal duties using its own resources, or is external assistance required? If the latter then how are external relations to be regulated?

Activity

You should now have a good idea of how you organise your department and the steps you might take to improve your skills.

Make a check-list of any changes you wish to make and devise a plan for implementing them.

Informal organisation

Large organisations consist of a number of smaller groups, each possessing its own organisational system. In particular, informal organisational structures arise, with coherent internal communication channels, group norms, perceptions and methods for allocating duties. Informal organisations are important because they sometimes develop goals and work routines contrary to the interests of the formal system. They often result from poor management/worker communication within the firm, for example:

- staff not knowing the organisation's true objectives
- absence of procedures for interdepartmental consultation and/or joint departmental decision taking
- a single favoured department dominating others, even to the extent that other departments feel they need its permission to undertake certain actions
- conflicts between individual and organisational objectives, including the pursuit of personal rather than company goals
- higher levels of management casually over-ruling decisions of subordinates. If senior managers do not back their juniors then the latter will conceal some of their activities and a hidden authority system may arise.

'Organisational development' (OD) can help in preventing informal systems usurping the official structure. OD is the process whereby management periodically and systematically audits the suitability of its existing organisation structure for meeting current needs. It examines the effectiveness of communications, employees' awareness of company goals and procedures, the efficiency of decision taking and the organisation's ability to respond to change. An important OD task is to identify individuals or small groups who, although believing that their actions are fully compatible with the organisation's formal aims, in fact steer the firm away from its proper objectives. Often, external rather than in-house 'agents of change' are better equipped to diagnose such problems, because the individuals and groups concerned have distorted perceptions of organisational needs. The change agent could be a member of the existing management, or an outside consultant hired specifically for the task. OD might involve training and management development, the creation of new departments and/or working groups and restructuring of departmental or

individual responsibilities. It is important that senior management be quite clear about what they expect from an OD
exercise and be willing to finance and implement its recommendations. There is little point in commissioning an (expensive)
OD survey if its findings are largely ignored!

Outside help is useful in OD because outsiders take a more
objective view of the organisation's activities and structural
requirements, and bring to the firm their experience of OD
exercises implemented elsewhere. Outside consultants have no
vested interests in the welfare of particular departments and are
not involved in internal departmental politics. The external
consultant needs to have immediate access to the highest levels
of management within the firm. OD is usually initiated at the
very top of an organisation and it is there that ultimate
responsibility for its success or failure must lie. Results from
OD investigations may have important implications for top
management and extensive structural reorganisation may be
required.

Activity

Organisational development is the process whereby management reviews its organisation structure.

Does your organisation conduct regular OD reviews? If so,
who conducts the review and what has been the outcome?

Few people would argue with the need to take a periodic look
at the structure of the organisation and assess whether it meets
current and future needs. However, it is time-consuming and it
may be difficult to implement the recommendations.

OD can analyse patterns of relationships within the firm and
their importance to the achievement of formal organisational
goals. Large groups contain sub-units, some of which are
permanent and officially recognised, others transitory and
arising purely to satisfy a passing need. Yet the personal
relationships created within temporary conditions; their sup-
portive nature and obvious relevance to practical and immediate problems, may cause them to persist long after the
original problems have been solved. In reality, organisational
'politics' can override patterns of relationships suggested by
firms' organisation charts or matrix structures. Groups form to

improve the relative power of sectional interests, staff and departments compete with each other informally for the attention of higher management, cliques, networks and alliances emerge — formal structures are undermined by unofficial organisational manoeuvres.

Summary

You are now in a position to take a critical look at the structure of your own organisation. For those working in small organisations, you will be able to consider the overall structure as well as that of your own area. If you work for a large organisation, with nationwide or even world-wide operations, a detailed study may be impossible. However, you should try to gather together as much information as you can.

See the extent to which you can apply the principles of good organisation structure to your own department and thereby improve your own management skills.

This chapter has concentrated on the practical aspects of organisation. The theory of organisation is considered further below.

Appendix — Organisational Theory

Supervisors are not expected to be expert management theoreticians. Nevertheless, you should be aware of the elements of organisational theory, and of its role in management theory. The major schools of thought in management studies are outlined in chapter 4. Here are described briefly some important theoretical and empirical contributions to the study of organisations, their structures and behaviour within them, beginning with a short account of the 'classical' school.

The classical theory of organisation is not the work of a single person, but an amalgam of the contributions of several (notably FW Taylor and Henri Fayol — see chapter 4) over many years. According to the classical approach, organisations should be designed to achieve specified objectives and personnel *then* allotted to various positions within the structure — people should be selected and trained to fit into the organisation; the organisation itself need not be structured to suit the human needs of particular individuals. Rigid organisational structures are recommended (cf bureaucracy) with individuals assigned to particular positions according to senior management's perceptions of their suitability for those posts. Jobs are not designed to suit particular individuals.

There is within a classical system much specialisation of work and division of functions, since by breaking activities down into simple standardised operations the speed and precision of those who perform them should increase. Less skill is required for easy repetitive administrative tasks, so fewer highly qualified employees need be employed. The classical approach thus recommends that each manager be responsible for a single function rather than for many diverse activities. Specialist skills then develop within the firm. This managerial division of labour creates the need for a pyramid structure of authority and control. At the apex of the pyramid is the managing director (or equivalent chief executive), followed by senior executives, line and staff managers, supervisors and, finally, operatives. Higher managers must coordinate the efforts of subordinates. The lower the manager's position in the hierarchy the more specialised the duties he or she will perform.

Another major tenet of the classical theory is the 'principle of exception', whereby subordinates are expected to submit to their superiors only brief, condensed reports on normal operations, but extensive analyses of deviations from past average performance or from the targets they were set by superiors. Routine matters are dealt with at low levels. Senior managers are thus left free to devote their time to unusual problems and major policy issues. Further principles of the classical theory are maintenance of unity of command and unbroken chain of command. Unity of command means that a subordinate should be directly responsible to one superior only and that instructions to the subordinate should not be issued from different sources, otherwise orders could conflict and the subordinate would have to choose which to obey. Practical application of this principle is difficult because of the strong influences that informal authority systems can sometimes exert. A person might in theory be responsible to a single superior, but in reality behave according to standards determined by someone else. The classical theory recommends narrow spans of control. It assumes that only small numbers of immediate subordinates can be efficiently managed by one superior. An unbroken 'chain of command' requires the existence of a clear line of authority running from the top of the managerial pyramid to its base. A break in the chain of command means that instructions issued by senior managers will not be implemented. Chaos and disruption might then ensue. Classical theory suggests that work be undertaken in clearly delineated departments, designed so as to specialise activities to the maximum extent.

Although organisations constructed along classical lines may be functionally efficient in some (important) respects, they might not be pleasant for employees and interpersonal communications difficulties created by rigid, formal and mechanistic structures could lead to operational inefficiencies in the longer term. 'Human behaviour' approaches to organisation (the principles of the human behaviour school of management thought are described in chapter 4) recommend participative management, focusing on the human and social needs of the individual employee. Job satisfaction, face-to-face relationships, consultation, joint activity and decision taking, flexibility and versatility are viewed as the crucial factors in organisational success. In designing organisations, management should seek to encourage personal initiative and creativity. Thus, rigid structures are to be avoided. There should be joint superior/subordinate determination of targets and close involvement of subordinates in the decision taking procedures that affect their daily working lives.

Human behaviour approaches have been criticised for their seemingly unrealistic altruism. Organisational needs and objectives can vary enormously depending on current environmental circumstances. Against backgrounds of fierce commercial competition, ideological concerns for personal development and individual human rights (laudable objectives in themselves) can appear implausible and naive. In particular, the existence of conflicts of interest in industry must be recognised. It is not necessarily the case that employees will feel they should pull together as a team. The 'contingency' approach to organisation insists that the general application of any single set of principles to organisational problems is bound to fail. Instead, organisations should be individually structured to meet the requirements of specific circumstances. The contingency approach is therefore the antithesis of the classical proposition that systems of authority and responsibility should be constant and predetermined.

Notes

1 Weber, M, *The Theory of Social and Economic Organisation*, Oxford University Press, New York, 1947.

3
Management by Objectives

Objectives

This chapter will help you to:

- understand the theory and practice of management by objectives
- implement the technique in order to achieve the benefits it can bring
- make the maximum use of management information systems.

Management by objectives (MBO) is at once a method of employee appraisal and a technique of organisational planning and control. It is a top down control technique whereby corporate objectives are segmented into departmental targets and then into objectives for individual employees. Superiors and subordinates meet and jointly agree subordinates' job specifications and goals, preferably in quantitative terms. MBO supposedly motivates employees through involving them in the determination of objectives, and should help them develop their individual careers. Subordinates who exceed their targets will experience a sense of satisfaction in their achievements. Causes of success can be isolated, analysed, and applied elsewhere. The concept is not new: in Britain it has been formally applied in military administration since 1914 — and informally since long before then. MBO imposes disciplined and logical approaches to decision taking. It forces managers to consider carefully the nature of their objectives, the factors affecting attainment of objectives, possible barriers, and all the alternatives available.

Origins of contemporary MBO

Three management theorists in particular have recommended the use of MBO in business situations. Peter Drucker's contribution is perhaps the best known.[1] According to Drucker, there are in business 'natural' forces militating against the emergence of common objectives. These 'factors of misdirection', Drucker argued, are managerial specialisation, hierarchical management structures and differences in the work and perceptions of individual managers. Thus, management should consciously seek to direct the activities of *all* the organisation's employees towards the attainment of one *common* goal and MBO would result in the integration of corporate and personal objectives. Managers would be able, he suggested, to control and improve their *own* performances since, in Drucker's words, 'self control means stronger motivation . . . higher performance and broader vision'.

John Humble saw MBO as a means for linking companies' desires for profits with managers' desires to contribute to decision making and to develop their careers.[2] He recommended a hierarchical system of objectives, initiated by the organisation's chief executive and starting from its corporate plan. Schemes should include targets for divisions, sections, departments and individuals. Action plans were needed, the preparation of which required systematic analysis of tasks and agreement on appropriate performance standards. Thus, managers should consult with subordinates to agree priorities and to establish the resources and authority needed to achieve objectives. This participative aspect of MBO caused Douglas McGregor to advocate consultative MBO systems.[3] In McGregor's view, an ideal MBO system would enable individuals

---

Self-check

How would you explain the concept of management by objectives?

Answer

Basically, it is an attempt to focus the activities of all members of staff towards achieving common goals. It is also argued that better results will be achieved if staff are actively involved in setting the objectives/targets to be reached.

to identify and pursue personal objectives in harmony with the needs of the enterprise. Through participation, managers appreciate the organisation's wider objectives and understand their personal contributions towards achieving them.

Once targets have been agreed, progress towards their attainment must be systematically monitored. This will be possible only if the targets set are clear and precise. Senior management is compelled, therefore, to elucidate its objectives, publicise them and pinpoint the criteria used in their formulation. Targets should be reasonably attainable, since unrealistic targets will never be met and, in consequence, the entire programme will fail.

Objectives can be specified at three levels: routine, developmental and for innovative effort. A sales manager, for example, might have a routine target of maintaining existing custom, a developmental target involving a launch of a new product and innovative targets concerned with location of new market opportunities, establishment of a new distribution system and the identification of demands for new goods. Objectives must be clearly defined: ambiguous phrases such as 'seeking to increase profits' or 'reducing costs' are inadequate. Targets must be specific and, if possible, expressed in numerical terms. What constitutes 'adequate' as opposed to 'excellent' performance should be explicitly stated. Impossibly high targets must be amended.

Employees require resources, authority and facilities in order to attain their targets. Resource requirements can be listed in MBO action plans drafted jointly by superior and subordinate which set out all the facilities, information and patterns of behaviour necessary for successful implementation of accepted objectives. The aim is to integrate the corporate goals of the firm with the personal aspirations of the individual manager, hopefully isolating those areas of his or her work that will enable individual effort to contribute most towards the attainment of broader company-wide objectives. At the end of each review period, employer and employee meet to ascertain how far the action plan has been implemented and to discuss difficulties encountered. Both parties suggest ways of improving performance and a further action plan for the next period is prepared. A convenient way to begin an action plan is with the superior making the statement, 'Your targets will be considered to have been met if . . .', and then filling in the rest of the sentence according to the requirements of the situation. The advantages of management by objectives are summarised below:

- it forces all employees to think carefully about their roles and objectives, about why tasks are necessary and how best to get things done
- targets are clarified and mechanisms are created for monitoring performance
- crucial elements are identified in each job. This information is useful for determining training and recruitment needs
- personal achievements of subordinates are recognised and rewarded
- superiors and subordinates are obliged to communicate. In consequence, superiors can quickly identify which subordinates are ready for promotion and the help they will need in preparing themselves for this
- performance is appraised against quantified targets, not subjective criteria
- there is forced coordination of activities, between departments, between junior and senior management, and between short and long term goals.

Activity

In theory, MBO can bring many benefits to the organisation but there can also be barriers. In the time allowed, identify as many problems as you can.

As you move on to the next section of the chapter, some of the problems associated with MBO are outlined. Compare these ideas with your own.

MBO systems require effective management information systems (see below) in order to assess the effects of subordinates' activities and the system should be sufficiently flexible to enable rapid revision of individual targets as environmental circumstances change. There are, of course, problems associated with MBO, including:

- the danger of meaningless attempts to quantify activities that are innately unquantifiable. How, for example, could the objectives of a manager whose role is purely advisory be expressed in numerical terms?

- possible encouragement of myopic emphasis on immediate quantifiable goals to the detriment of nebulous but nonetheless important longer-term objectives
- difficulties created through subordinates not being given the information, resources or authority necessary for completion of tasks allocated to them
- the enormous amount of time consumed by regular consultations between higher and lower executives. A dictatorial system whereby superiors simply impose targets on subordinates, without consultation, might be more efficient. Moreover, firms operating in highly uncertain, rapidly changing market environments may need to alter their objectives so frequently that MBO procedures become impractical
- tendencies of senior managers to pay more attention to subordinates' personal qualities than to the work done by them
- possible concentration of effort on the achievement of individual rather than departmental targets.

MBO at the departmental level

If you have to implement a management by objectives programme you will need to draft a precise and comprehensive statement of your departmental aims. Do this yourself, but send copies to all the people who work for you and to your immediate superior together with a covering memorandum asking for comment. Emphasise in the memorandum that your statement represents only your own personal and provisional

---

Activity

How did your list of problems compare with that given in the text? Many of the difficulties are connected with the attitude of staff and the lack of accurate information. Since an MBO exercise is time consuming and costly, there can be a reluctance to rethink the plan in light of current economic events.

Your organisation may already use MBO. As you read on, the text concentrates on implementing MBO at the departmental level.

Try to follow the procedure outlined.

view, and that it *will* be amended following discussions. Split the statement into two sections — one for the 'central aim' of the department, the other for 'specific objectives'. The central aim is a statement of the reason for your department's existence. It should relate directly to wider organisational aims dictated by higher levels of authority. Without a clearly specified central aim it is impossible to determine particular tasks that need to be done and the resources and authority necessary for their completion. If you cannot specify what you want your department to achieve, you will not be able to define meaningful targets for subordinates.

Hold a briefing session to inform your colleagues of the existence of the exercise. Then have a departmental meeting at which each subordinate can present his or her own interpretation of the central aim. Identify differences in various peoples' perceptions of this (write out the contrasting interpretations on a wall chart or flip pad if you have one) and have your subordinates openly state their views. A representative from senior management should be present in order to arbitrate whenever serious disagreements emerge. It is appropriate for a senior management representative to be present since he or she can relate the various interpretations of the department's role presented at the meeting to fundamental organisational goals. At the end of the meeting you should have an agreed position about what the department exists to do. It is very difficult to run a department whose members cannot concur on its basic purpose. If agreement cannot be reached, senior management will have to impose a settlement.

After the meeting, write out a list of all the tasks that will have to be done to achieve the central aim and alongside each item write a prediction of the consequences for the central aim if that task is not completed satisfactorily. Ensure that each task relates directly to the central aim. Now allocate these tasks to various employees according to your opinion of their ability to undertake them. List the skills and experience needed to perform tasks, noting the personal strengths and weaknesses of the individuals to whom particular tasks have been allocated. Discuss the allocations with each subordinate, in private, on a one-to-one basis. Negotiate acceptance of specific achievement targets, noting subordinates' reservations and objections. You need to ensure that *someone* has a target relating to *every single objective*. Record this action plan formally in a typewritten document and file it for future reference.

Self-check

Distinguish between the 'central aim' of the department and 'specific objectives'.

Answer

Central aim: a general statement, giving the broad purpose of the department.

Specific objective: usually based on the 'central aim' and identifying the tasks to be done, the resources needed etc.

Management audits

Policies and procedures are effective in achieving organisational aims only if they relate to targets and to be relevant they must be up to date. Management auditing is the term used to describe the systematic analysis of the efficiency of policies adopted and procedures applied in attaining goals. Audits should be comprehensive (looking at all aspects of the firm's operations and not just some of them) and regular. As well as undertaking audits at predetermined intervals (say once every two or three years for a thorough investigation), audits are needed whenever external situations or internal circumstances significantly change. Business environments are dynamic in nature — they evolve, alter unexpectedly, generate new opportunities and make irrelevant some existing activities. The purpose of a major audit is to reorganise resources — material, financial and human — and redirect effort towards the more efficient attainment of currently pressing organisational goals. Minor audits, taking one department at a time, might be completed between major analyses. Large firms sometimes hire outside consultants to conduct management audits, on the grounds that outsiders will be more objective in their approach.

Auditing, planning, MBO and performance appraisal are all parts of the same package of management activity. Planning and the specification of departmental and individual targets have meaning only if current administrative procedures are adequate for implementing the targets set. Two types of audit are needed: internal and external. External audits examine the

general environments, legal (the effects of changes in employment law for example), economic, market opportunities,
behaviour of competitors etc that surround the organisation.
Internal audits investigate operational systems inside the enterprise and are the type of audit with which executive managers
are usually concerned. Often, checklists are issued to department heads in order to gather information on the relevance of
sectional activities, on the flow of work through sections and
on relationships between resource inputs and departmental
productivity. Standard work study techniques are frequently
used to analyse efficiency during audits. A typical audit will
examine such things as:

- management style and communications
- whether organisation charts and job specifications are up
  to date
- whether organisational and departmental objectives are
  understood by all department members
- possible duplication of activities
- operational efficiency with sections
- plant and/or office layout.

Monitoring activity

Setting targets is not of itself sufficient to ensure that an
organisation will function efficiently. Organisations need to be
controlled, ie monitored to ensure that targets are met. You
need to establish what information needs to be collected for
control purposes, by whom it should be gathered and when.
Note how much time and money might be spent on compiling
control data. It is essential therefore that the information
collected has a definite and valuable use. In general, the less
expensive the control process the better, so that automatic
control systems requiring only minimal human intervention are
normally preferred. Control has three aspects: information
input, data evaluation and feedback to the controlling authority. Rapid feedback is essential. Otherwise problems could
develop faster than the controller's ability to correct them.
Obviously, corrective action should always be taken when
targets are not achieved. What is the point of installing a
control mechanism only to ignore the deficiencies it reveals?

Ultimate responsibility for control necessarily lies with top
management, which will delegate appropriate control duties.

Self-check

What is meant by a management audit and how does it fit in with MBO?

Answer

Management audit is the systematic analysis of the efficiency of policies adopted and procedures applied in attaining goals. The audit is split into two parts: internal, looking at the operational systems within the organisation; and external, looking at the environment in which the organisation operates.

The audit is a prerequisite to setting objectives.

The first stage in the control process is to use information gathered from a management audit to describe all current activities. This constitutes the *input* of the system, which is then compared with existing targets and, if necessary, corrective action is taken or targets amended to more realistic levels. Problems inevitably occur, among them the possibilities that:

- current activities might not be reported accurately, comprehensively, or in sufficient detail
- inappropriate criteria might have been used in setting initial performance objectives, resulting in unattainable targets which render the entire system inoperable
- historical records of relevant activities may be inadequate
- information retrieval systems could be faulty.

Control methods

Control processes link inputs to outputs and provide feedback. They measure current activities, compare them with activities specified in plans and correct deviations from predetermined norms. Managers are likely to encounter three methods of practical control: budgeting, compilation and analysis of control ratios and the analysis of costs. Budgeting and costing are dealt with in chapter 7 and various key ratios are discussed under the subject headings to which they relate. There are, however, a number of general comments on ratio analysis that are worth making at this point.

> **Activity**
>
> Control processes are important as they provide feedback and enable actual achievements to be measured and compared with targets set in the management plan. Any deviation must be investigated.
>
> What control methods does your organisation use and how are they implemented?

Ratio analysis

Preparation and monitoring of operational ratios permits the comparison of relative performance figures (rather than absolute amounts) over time. Each department must choose the ratios most relevant to its needs. A credit control department for instance will be interested in the ratio of bad debts to sales, while production managers will want to measure (among others) ratios of costs to outputs and average inventory to purchases. Personnel specialists will compute labour turnover indices (eg the number of employees with more than one year's service divided by the total number of people employed one year ago) and figures for revenue per person employed. Other important ratios are value added per employee, wage cost per unit of production, actual performance divided by target performance (for various variables) and value added per unit of plant or machinery.

'Normal' values for key ratios may be predetermined and acceptable deviations specified. Management by exception procedures can then be applied. Ratio analysis has much to offer as a technique of management control, since ratios can be used to show interrelationships between functional activities and large volumes of data can be summarised into a few easily understood figures. Note however that a ratio consists of both a numerator *and* a denominator — an increase in one has an effect equivalent to a decrease in the other. Thus, a ratio that is reasonably constant over time might conceal large but counterbalancing disturbances in the variables that make up the ratio and these movements might be important and deserve close investigation.

A ratio should be relevant to the purpose for which it is intended and should be computed consistently. Where data definitions vary, ratios calculated using different criteria should not be compared. Different firms measure variables in contrasting ways. Accordingly, cross firm or industry ratio comparisons ought not to be attempted unless comparable measurement techniques are guaranteed. Some firms value stock at cost, others at replacement value; some firms use straightline methods for depreciating fixed asset values, others use the method of diminishing balance. Ratios should not be interpreted in isolation, but compared with norms or targets and their constituent elements periodically examined in depth.

Feedforward and feedback

A good control system will be flexible and thus capable of easy adjustment as circumstances change. Environments, corporate objectives and organisational climates alter over time — market conditions change, competing firms enter and leave industries. Equally, a control system should be clear and easily understood by those who use it: complicated formulae, statistics, graphs etc can obscure simple issues.

Flexible, understandable systems will generate feedback informing controllers of the consequences of their decisions. Feedback, however, is retrospective — when the information arrives it may be too late to remedy malfunctions. It is better, therefore, that control processes contain predictive elements so that future problems can be forecast in advance and measures taken now to overcome them. Accordingly, control theorists increasingly focus their attention on feedforward, as opposed to feedback, systems. These are 'future orientiated', meaning that current activities are altered today according to forecasts of future events. In other words, likely eventualities are predicted and policies introduced now to overcome the difficulties they might cause. Thus, for example, management might predict today that future sales will fall because of increased marketing activity by a major competitor. Consequently, the firm alters its marketing policies, increases its advertising and public relations expenditure and generally intensifies its selling efforts to counteract the forecast decline in sales. Whereas feedback systems concentrate on initiating remedial actions at the output stage, feedforward schemes centre on decision making in the input period. If inputs differ from activities necessary to overcome predicted difficulties, they are altered in appropriate ways.

The success of a feedforward system depends ultimately on the accuracy of forecasts and business forecasts in particular are notoriously unreliable. There are so many variables involved: alterations in public taste, government policy, behaviour of competitors etc and all are liable to change at any time.

Self-check

What is the main drawback with a feedback system of control and how can a feedforward system overcome the problem?

Answer
Feedback is retrospective, ie gives information concerning the consequences of decisions taken. Therefore, little can be done to remedy the situation.

Feedforward incorporates predictive elements so that current activities are amended in light of forecasts of future events.

Monitoring techniques

You can adopt various approaches to the monitoring function. The essential choice is between continuous involvement or the adoption of an arm's length 'management by exception' (MBE) approach. The latter was first advocated by F W Taylor in his book, *The Principles of Scientific Management*, published in 1911. Subordinates, Taylor argued, should submit to their superiors only brief, condensed reports on normal operations, but extensive reports on deviations from past average performance or targets set by higher management. Once established, standards should be monitored through picking out significant deviations from predetermined norms. Exceptionally good or bad results would be analysed in depth, but reasonable deviations from standard performance would not be questioned. Thus, routine matters would be dealt with at lower levels, leaving higher-level managers free to devote their time to unusual problems and policy issues.

Management by exception has been popular because of the enormous volume of information continuously generated within firms and the physical impossibility of continuously monitoring actual activities. Thus, data could be collected continuously but analysed periodically (weekly, monthly, quarterly, annually). By specifying tolerable deviations from target performance and intervening only if the limits of tolerable deviation were exceeded, management could avoid becoming immersed in trivial issues and instead reserve its time and efforts for more demanding problems.

There are, however, several difficulties associated with MBE. First, there are time lags between the moment a problem arises, the moment it is noticed and the time remedial action is implemented. Manufacturing cost data, for example, may be collated and analysed once a month; if a particular production line develops a fault and begins to generate unacceptably high expenses at the start of the month, the situation will not be recognised until the month's end. Then there is a further delay before a report goes to higher management, followed by another lag until corrective action is taken and during these delays high extra costs are being incurred. The second major problem is that since 'acceptable' deviations from target performance are tolerated without investigation, it is possible for a particular activity to be perpetually above or below standard by a relatively small amount without the fact ever being reported. Hence minor defects continue and overall performance is constantly lower than could be the case. Equally, the cause of consistently superior performance just below the upper reporting boundary will not be examined; there is no mechanism for isolating the factors contributing to high achievement and applying these factors elsewhere.

Continuous monitoring, on the other hand, is today much easier than it was because of the availability of increasingly powerful desktop computer systems. Information on costs, outputs, revenues and other relevant variables can be immediately analysed at the moment of collection and existing summaries can be updated at once. Trends in costs and outputs can be picked up, hour by hour, as they occur. Managers in control of a computerised system can requisition information at will and order its presentation in any one of a variety of alternative forms.

Problems are highlighted instantly – they will be observed on the appropriate manager's visual display unit whenever he or she types into the system a command to update information on current activities. Production lines which begin to produce defectives; labour and materials costs which start to get out of hand; increasing overheads; falling sales etc can be identified as they happen so that remedial action can be applied at once.

Original accounting documents such as invoices, credit notes, sales vouchers and cheques received and paid, may simultaneously be recorded and integrated into the input data for the program which prepares the firm's final accounts. Interim statements of these accounts will be available instantly.

In a non-computerised system, monitoring may be undertaken in several ways. You must accept that the time and cost of collecting useful information requires you to be highly selective in the data you collate. First, decide *which* targets you most want to monitor and assess the cost of control (collecting figures, meetings, discussions with subordinates etc). Ask yourself what would happen if you did not bother monitoring specific activities? What questions will the information collected answer and are those questions really worthwhile? Then you must decide how to gather the information — whether to do it yourself or delegate the task to a subordinate. In the latter case you must issue clear and precise instructions about how, when and where the data are to be collected and you need to ensure that the person to whom you entrust the responsibility is reliable and competent at these tasks.

Activity

Information is essential if managers are to perform their duties efficiently. The more accurate and up-to-date the information, the better the managers will be able to plan, organise, control and coordinate.

Take a few minutes to study the information system your organisation uses to collect, store and retrieve data.

It is highly likely that the computer will feature in your MIS.

As you read on you will see some of the modern techniques available.

Management information systems

An efficient management information system (MIS) will enable management to plan, coordinate, organise and control its activities. Information systems collect, store and retrieve data. In the past, the volume of data handled within a system has been constrained by limitations on available clerical labour and the inability of many people to comprehend and assimilate large quantities of information. Hence, various summary statistics were developed to ease the burdens of data collection and interpretation. Likewise, many financial accounting procedures have been designed to enable easy checking of the accuracy of bookkeeping entries and to facilitate periodic extraction of summary data on sales, creditors, discounts received and given and so on. Aggregate figures only were available, however, because of the difficulties and expenses of cross-tabulation. Comprehensive detailed analyses with respect to various categories and subheadings were not generally possible.

Computerisation has cut the costs of data collection and has made easy the reduction of large amounts of data into summary numbers. Cross-tabulation has become effortless and the precise form in which data are presented can be chosen at will. A great benefit of computerised data processing is the integration at source of each piece of information into the management control system of the entire organisation. Data are recorded once but then used for many different purposes in different departments. Thus, information on production costs will be diffused simultaneously to the accounts department, production planning and control, costing department, the purchasing manager, stores and stock controllers and any other interested party. The data will be presented to each of these recipients in a form which is precisely relevant to their particular needs. It is not necessary for several departments to collect and prepare what is essentially the same information.

This has implications for the structure of departmentalisation within the firm, since many functions which previously were independent may, with the assistance of an integrated data presentation network, be combined.

The installation of an MIS might, at first sight, appear to be a relatively straightforward task. There are only a few factors to consider — when, how and to whom information should be transmitted and how best to summarise data in a form that enables fast and accurate evaluation prior to taking decisions. In practice, however, difficulties emerge, including the following:

- relevant information might not reach the right people. Managers commonly assume that colleagues and subordinates have been informed of particular facts when, actually, they have not. Transmission of every piece of information that might be relevant to an individual is not feasible; otherwise the firm would devote all its time, energy and resources to transmitting messages, most of which were of little practical use. Thus, choices have to be made, and dangers exist that the wrong people will receive information

- breaks in the chain of command. Information should flow vertically through the enterprise from its top to its bottom via channels illustrated in its organisation chart. Often, information bottlenecks occur at supervisory and middle management levels since supervisors and middle managers not only receive information from above (and have to decide whether to act on it) but also collect feedback from lower levels. If a supervisor fails to act on relevant information received, the chain of command is broken — policies are not implemented; feedback on the success or failure of policies is not transmitted to higher authority

- horizontal flows of information among colleagues of equal rank may be interrupted if certain individuals deliberately conceal information or, through incompetence, do not pass it on.

The effectiveness of an MIS should be evaluated against its ability to assist in taking decisions: operations decisions, long and short term planning, budgeting, investment decisions, and so on. Information generated is often used to compare things (costs, alternative possibilities, environmental circumstances, etc) in new and meaningful ways. There is little point in creating extra information the substance of which is already known. Strategic information needed for long range planning must often be obtained from external sources, and involve market and marketing research,[4] as well as the analysis of macroeconomic indicators, investigation of outside sources of supply of labour, raw materials, finance etc. Such information may be extremely inaccurate and should be treated with caution. Internally generated information used for tactical decision making and operational control should, in principle, not contain serious errors. Records of output, expenditures, wage payments, labour turnover and so on result from written reports, direct observation, face to face or telephone messages or from completion of check lists or questionnaires, but even these data might be flawed. Miscounting of items is common, delays occur in registering information contained in documents (invoices for example), while questionnaires and check lists, however well designed, may be quickly and haphazardly completed on the shop floor.

Records have to be organised into categories. Increasingly, information is categorised and stored in 'databases' operated from a desktop computer.

Self-check

What does the term 'database' mean to you?

Answer
Database is a technical term applied to a type of computer software that categorises and stores information. The simplest example of a database is the names and addresses of customers. This information is stored on the computer database and used for mass mail shots, identifying those customers who live in a given town etc.

In the next section of the chapter you will be given a more detailed explanation of how a database is constructed and how it can be used.

Databases

A database (DB) is a pool of information. A DB program (of which there are several varieties) will sort that information into predetermined categories, select and display items according to one or more criteria, perform mathematical functions on data and present information in some chosen form (lists, bar charts or pie diagrams, report formats, financial accounts etc). Modern programs, even the least expensive can hold so many entries (the simplest can store at least 75,000 items) that capacity is not a limiting factor. Rather, the functions to be performed determine the requirements of an appropriate DB system for a particular firm.

Information on (say) all a firm's customers can be put into a customer *file*. Similar files can be created around other aspects of the business. The DB itself is the aggregate of these files. A *record* is a self contained set of information within a file. Suppose for example you had a file of names and addresses of customers, then each name and address would be a separate record. The records themselves are made up of *fields*. Thus, in a name and address, the name is one field and the postcode another. You must define your fields carefully because they are used to identify particular records. If for instance you have a separate field for the town in each address then later on you will be able to extract all addresses within any specified town.

The most expensive databases have a relational facility whereby one file is related to another. For example, you could relate customers' names and addresses to how much each customer purchased from you during the previous year, or a file for salespeoples' orders could be related to a file for the expenses they claim. A search of a database is undertaken across one or more fields, such as, 'All customers in London with names beginning with the letter A and who spent more than £100 with this company last year'. The cheaper the program, the fewer fields can be examined at any one time. More expensive systems (though none cost more than a couple of hundred pounds) offer, in effect, self-contained MIS record keeping facilities.

Information within a DB can be organised 'dimensionally' as well as 'hierarchically'. To conceptualise this idea, think of a hierarchical information system as a tree, with a main trunk, branches, twigs and leaves. There is only one route to each leaf, via the trunk, branch and twig system. In a relational system, however, you can go not only to a single leaf, but to any number of them simultaneously. Thus, for example, a garage stock control system would, using a hierarchical system, identify stock *first* by assembly type (bodywork, electrics etc), *then* by subassembly (doors, lighting, ignition and so on), *then* by make of car and *finally* by specific part. With a relational stock control system on the other hand you do not need to go through this tedious information gathering procedure. The order in which you identify the features of an item can be reversed or mixed up and still lead to the correct component. In this particular example, the problem is how to reorder, automatically, many parts for many models from many suppliers. Here, you would simply create three files: a stock item file; a suppliers' file with suppliers' names, addresses, prices, terms etc; a purchase order file containing past details and who can supply them. Each time a part is recorded as having been withdrawn from stock, the stock item file will be automatically updated and if the withdrawal causes stocks of that item to fall below a preset limit then, via relational linkages to the other fields, a supplier will be identified and a purchase order with the supplier's name and address automatically printed out.

Spreadsheets

Increasingly, database information is inputted from 'spreadsheets'. A spreadsheet is simply a grid containing data and formulae which processes the data. It performs functions that could not be achieved using manual methods, even with calculators. The common analogy is to compare spreadsheets with accounting ledgers, except that the spreadsheet does all the adding and subtracting, juxtaposition of entries etc instantly and automatically. Spreadsheets can be used, moreover, for nearly all other management information applications. The concept predates computers; accountants long ago devised standardised specially lined paper to assist inexperienced clerks prepare accounting statements, but the hard arithmetic then had to be done by hand. Following the arrival of personal computers it soon became possible to purchase electronic spreadsheets which not only organised data in predetermined ways, but which also did the arithmetic. The calculating speed and power of a computer was combined with spreadsheet layouts.

A computer based spreadsheet comprises a matrix of cells (entries) located by horizontal and vertical grid references. Data can be moved around and arithmetically manipulated. Subtotals can be extracted at will. A particularly useful attribute of the modern electronic spreadsheet is its ability to complete 'what if' projections at the touch of a button, ie you can change your assumptions about various factors and observe the effects. For example, if your spreadsheet has been programmed to calculate the manufacturing cost of an item you can ask the question, 'What if labour costs increase by five per cent and the cost of raw material falls by two per cent?', and receive an answer at once since the computer will automatically and instantly recalculate all the relevant figures. Output from spreadsheets can often be used as input to files in other programs, and information may be presented graphically as well as in lists and tables and preformatted reports. Spreadsheets are today widely used in industry and commerce for accounting, statistical analyses, financial modelling, cash flow forecasting and business planning generally.

Decision support systems

The term 'decision support system' (DSS) is used to describe the collection of computing tools used to solve problems and take decisions. Examples of the components of a decision support system include databases and spreadsheets, graphics packages, and programs for statistical analysis and the manipulation of data. The aim is to be able to call up and instantly analyse large quantities of data, possibly conducting 'what if' and other sensitivity analyses to predict the likely consequences of various courses of action. Note that the DSS is *not* the same as a management information system. The latter collates, stores and retrieves data, but does not require those who operate it to exercise judgement or discretion. Operation of a DSS, conversely, demands the manipulation and interpretation of information and the logical structuring of decision making tasks.

Recent developments in the DSS/MIS field have focused on 'end user computing', which involves designing computer packages and systems in such a way that they can be manipulated and their outputs adapted by employees who have no special qualifications or expertise in computing or IT. End user computing is becoming an important subject in its own right, and software and systems are increasingly being reformated, in order to give the non-specialist package user maximum discretion in determining the nature of the information generated by the system. End user computing has many implications for supervisory management, especially in white-collar situations. Routine decision-making becomes much faster and there is greater need for staff who are capable of assessing the reliability of outputs from systems that contain information on topics with which they are not familiar. White-collar jobs become more interesting as employees take on the role of choosing *how* they complete IT related tasks. This provides

---

Activity

The preceding section talked about spreadsheets. If this is the first time you have heard of this term, you should certainly make a note to learn more about it. Once you have mastered the technique, this piece of software can assist almost every manager in the planning and organising process.

numerous possibilities for job enrichment. Moreover, there is a levelling out of the performance levels of the best and worst employees, since the computer will do a lot of the employee's basic work. The need for expert staff diminishes.

Summary

Management by objectives places great importance on the setting of targets, monitoring results and comparing the two. It also seeks to bring all the parts of the organisation together by giving them common goals to work towards.

While your organisation may not adhere to this theory in total, some elements of it are likely to be used.

If you are unfamiliar with some of the control techniques mentioned and the computer software, it is up to you to remedy this. There are still some managers who are unwilling or unable to make full use of computers.

Identify the techniques you wish to adopt and the computer software you wish to use, and draw up an action plan to acquire the necessary expertise.

Notes

1 Drucker, P F, *The Practice of Management*, Heinemann, London, 1955.
2 Humble, J, *Management by Objectives in Action*, McGraw-Hill, Maidenhead, 1970.
3 McGregor, D, *The Human Side of Enterprise*, McGraw-Hill, New York, 1960.
4 Market research concerns the analysis of the geographic and socio-economic structure of markets. Marketing research is research into any aspect of marketing: consumer behaviour, effectiveness of advertising, salesforce appraisal etc.

4

Management Style

Objectives

At the end of this chapter you will be able to:

- explain the advantages and disadvantages of the different styles of leadership
- evaluate the theories on leadership style.

Management is a process that seeks to achieve the objectives of organisations in the most efficient ways possible. It is concerned therefore with the design of organisations, their structure and development, the specification of organisational objectives and choice of criteria for evaluating organisational efficiency. Management sets targets, imposes budgets, plans, controls, coordinates, leads and motivates staff and takes decisions. It monitors performance and initiates remedial action when plans are not achieved. Strategic decision making is the concern of owners, directors and other very senior managers. Strategy concerns the broad directions the organisation should follow. For example, what products should the firm produce? Which unions should be recognised? How is the firm to finance its operations? What prices should it charge? Tactical management is the *implementation* of strategic decisions, and as such is the responsibility of executive managers. It involves the deployment of resources, work allocation, monitoring workflows and reporting back to higher authority. Executives take decisions and coordinate workplace activities; they issue instructions to subordinates, motivate them to increased efforts and monitor their performances.

Activity

Make a list of the duties performed by management.

The actual functions performed by management will vary from organisation to organisation and from level to level. However, the basic duties of management involve decision-making, planning, organising, problem-solving and controlling. You may have identified specific tasks, based on your own experience.

Management

Management involves planning, organising, coordinating and control. It may be divided into line activities such as marketing or production and service functions (personnel, method study etc) needed to ensure that line activities are actually carried out. Much management work is to do with taking decisions and improving efficiency, including the efficiency of the management process itself. Some management techniques rely entirely on personal expertise (eg negotiation, giving orders, delegation), others involve administrative abilities, such as competence in written communications or the processing of documents.

In a limited company, strategy is determined by the firm's board of directors which is elected by shareholders to protect their interests. Directors may be full time or part time. Full time (executive directors) are employees of the firm and control particular functions such as marketing or personnel. Part time (non-executive) board members act as consultants, bringing specialist skills and wide ranging experience to the board. Day by day involvement with functional operations means that full time directors possess expert detailed knowledge of the firm, but they may not be as impartial and objective in assessing the company's prospects as are those who work for the board part time. However, part time directors might not be as committed to the organisation as their full time colleagues.

Supervisory managers are primarily concerned with the implementation of senior management's decisions and with interpersonal skills and the procedural aspects of administration. As an executive you plan, control and organise, are partially involved in recruitment, training, induction and other personnel activities, and contribute indirectly to a wide range of specialist functions.

A typical manager's duties will include the planning and progressing of work, quality management (including inspection), induction and training, counselling and appraisal of subordinates, grievance control and all the matters discussed in other chapters. Management is a demanding activity — not only do you need to know about a wide range of subjects, but you also face widely diverse and possibly conflicting demands on your time. For example, while production executives are asking for more output, quality controllers might insist on better work standards. Engineers may want a product made in a way that increases costs, while financial executives may simultaneously request that manufacturing costs be minimised.

You may have been appointed directly to a management post, or promoted from the ranks of the group you are then expected to manage. The latter situation might cause problems, since you will probably have been promoted as much for your performance in your previous job as for your ability to control others. You may have been an excellent operative, salesperson, bank clerk or whatever, but without conscious effort (reading this book for example) you might not be equally competent in the skills and practices of executive management. Existing technical competencies which you diligently acquired over many years may cease to be important, while new competencies — interviewing, delegation, influencing people, negotiation, performance appraisal, setting objectives etc — are needed.

Hopefully, your firm will recognise the importance of management skills training, realising that to entrust a team of people to an untrained, inept manager is as dangerous and potentially costly as entrusting the operation of valuable equipment to unskilled and incompetent manual workers.

Effective managers are good at communication and able to turn their hand to a variety of activities. Excessively introspective, standoffish individuals rarely become effective executives — you *must* learn to work with others and adopt flexible, quickly responsive attitudes to change. Try to broaden your horizons. Learn as much as you can about other departments

Activity

Identify the levels of management within your organisation and for each level summarise the tasks performed. Try to think in general terms, rather than specific jobs.

The number of levels will vary, but they are simplified into four basic groups:

Top Level — Board of Directors.
Long term objectives and goals. Broad direction of the organisation.

Senior Level — Heads of Department
Strategies for achieving long term goals. Broad direction for individual departments. Resources needed.

Middle Level — Heads of Section
Short term objectives leading to achieving long term goals. Preparation of budgets and control of activities. Efficient use of resources.

Supervisory Level
People management on a daily basis. Short term targets and resources needed to meet targets.

Clearly, this is a generalisation and there will be a degree of overlap. Information must flow down the structure and feedback up the structure.

and their personnel and establish contacts with your opposite numbers in these other departments.

How you manage your department will result from your personal inclinations, your training and environmental factors. It should depend also on a conscious decision about your management style and, in particular, your pattern of leadership. You choose the clothes you wear, you choose the food you eat, there is no reason at all why you should not equally choose a particular mode of management behaviour! Managers, remember, are judged not by the work they produce as individuals but by their ability to achieve results through the efforts of a team. Your choice of style must therefore be geared to its effects on the morale and hence the productivity of your department.

The style of management a person adopts affects his or her relations with subordinates and (importantly) the patterns of interaction among them. Do not expect to be included in informal departmental get-togethers or to be told stories 'through the grapevine'. As a supervisor, you are an integral and important part of the *management* system, representing managerial interests and required to implement *managerial* decisions. You are not a union representative — if you were then you would be fully justified in devoting yourself completely to the furtherance of the union cause. Nor are you an intermediary between management and workers. You do not arbitrate industrial disputes, or represent employees in grievances against the organisation. These matters, important as they are, are someone else's responsibility. Your task is to speak for management, and management alone — naive attempts to reconcile widely divergent and conflicting interests between management and labour will cause you distress and are bound, ultimately, to fail.

Leadership

Your subordinates will expect you to lead the department. You are, after all, the appointed manager and leadership is an integral component of the supervisory role. Accordingly, you need to choose a leadership style, depending on your personality, inclinations, the character of your subordinates and their working environment.

Activity

What style of leadership do you adopt? How would you describe it to a new member of staff?

It does not matter if you do not use the accepted terminology. Essentially, you have to decide on the degree to which you are autocratic or democratic, impose decisions or consult, and whether you exercise strict control or delegate responsibility.

You may say that you have to adapt your style of leadership to meet different situations, but in this case identify the approach you use most often.

Perhaps you should also ask yourself, which approach would you like to adopt, and why are you unable to do so?

As you read on, you will gain some further insight into the theories on leadership styles.

Between the extremes of complete autocracy and, conversely, a totally democratic mode of leadership there is a continuum of possible approaches. You might for example consult your staff when considering problems, while reserving all final decisions for yourself, you could impose your decisions without comment or discussion or you may resolve issues totally democratically via free votes.

Leadership has been extensively investigated by writers on management style. Different phrases are used to describe various approaches, though all mean essentially the same. FE Fiedler, for example, distinguishes between 'permissive' and 'directive' modes of behaviour.[1] RE Blake and J Mouton refer to 'concern for people' as opposed to 'concern for production'.[2] R Likert describes 'job centred' versus 'employee centred' management.[3] Other phrases used to define these concepts have included 'task orientated' (ie autocratic) and 'people centred' (democratic) styles, 'tight' and 'flexible', 'cooperative' versus 'dictatorial' and so on.

Ultimately you have to decide whether to supervise your subordinates closely, issuing precise and detailed instructions covering every task, or whether to specify overall objectives and leave subordinates to achieve them as they think fit. Autocratic styles (associated usually with tight and comprehensive supervision) can be dictatorial or paternalistic. The former approach involves rewards and penalties (often in the form of a steeply progressive bonus system), threats of sanctions for underperformance, highly formal interpersonal relationships and, generally, strict control. Paternalistic styles similarly involve detailed supervision, though the leader tries consciously to capture the allegiance and respect of subordinates through the force of his or her personality. Favours are bestowed on those who adhere to the leader's wishes; dissent is tolerated, though not condoned. Subordinates are not expected to exercise initiative, indeed they are actively discouraged from doing so. Consequently, subordinates are never allowed to develop their decision making and leadership potential, with the result that work in the department effectively ceases whenever the leader is away.

Democratic approaches can be consultative or laissez-faire. Subordinates participate to varying degrees in planning, decision taking and control, and there is much consultation and communication. Whereas the autocratic leader 'tells' subordinates about decisions (possibly 'selling' decisions as well), the democratic leader involves subordinates in the decision taking process. With laissez-faire leadership, subordinates are left completely alone to make whatever decisions they deem necessary to achieve their objectives. Consultation implies (but does not guarantee) joint decision taking between workers and the group leader, though the latter will try his or her utmost to persuade workers to accept a particular point of view. This can improve workers' morale, stimulate their initiative and, through broadening their responsibilities, increase workers' job satisfaction. On the other hand, continual disagreement and lack of positive direction might prevent objectives being attained. The analysis of leadership behaviour has a long and varied history. Leadership ability in individuals is easy to recognise and it has long been accepted that actual (as opposed to nominal) leadership in work situations is often exercised by unofficial leaders. However, the precise identification of the factors that cause certain people to become good leaders — to be able to alter the opinions and behaviour of others — is difficult.

Self-check

The autocratic style of leadership may be described as dictatorial or paternalistic, and the democratic style consultative or laissez-faire. Distinguish between these terms.

Answer
The autocratic approach involves precise instructions to staff, close control and little delegation. If you are dictatorial you achieve results by rewards and penalties (more often the latter) and through fear. With the paternalistic approach you try to gain the respect of subordinates and tend to concentrate on rewarding acceptable behaviour rather than punishing dissent.

The democratic style attempts to involve subordinates in the decision-making process. While the consultation process does not guarantee that the views of the subordinates will be acted upon, the laissez-faire approach abdicates management responsibility.

Three major categories of leadership theory exist: trait, human behaviour and contingency. Trait theories have long been discarded by most people — though the ideas rooted in them still persist in the more remote and backward corners of industry. They assert that leadership ability is an innate personal characteristic, ie that certain individuals are born as 'natural' leaders. According to this view, people who are good at leadership possess certain inbred qualities, and the task of management is to identify persons with these qualities and allot them to leadership posts.

Relevant personality traits might include initiative, decisiveness, self-assurance, assertiveness, intelligence, desire for occupational achievement and desire for financial reward. It has even been argued that a person's dress, stature and physical appearance can affect leadership ability. The biggest problem with trait theory is perhaps the huge number of personality characteristics potentially relevant to good leadership. Moreover, even assuming that certain traits do affect leadership ability it is doubtful whether they can be objectively measured. How, for example, can 'enthusiasm' or 'self-assurance' be quantified? Identification of characteristics is necessarily subjective and the choice of leaders becomes correspondingly haphazard.

Activity

List the qualities/traits a good leader should possess.

You have probably included qualities such as good communication skills, initiative, self-assurance, gets on well with people, able to command respect, sound technical knowledge.

While it is difficult to argue against the need for such skills, the problem is whether they can be objectively measured. The qualities we see as desirable are usually influenced by our own concept of what constitutes a good leader.

Are these qualities in-born, or can they be acquired? A question for you to ponder before continuing with the chapter.

Trait theory insists that individuals either do or do not possess the characteristics of a good leader. The 'behaviour' approach, in contrast, asserts that leadership ability, far from being innate, is a quality that can be taught and learned! Good leadership, behaviourists argue, depends on how leaders behave, so that instruction in appropriate forms of behaviour can be given to people appointed to leadership roles. Rensis Likert, the American psychologist referred to above, defined 'job centred' leadership as that which involved the close supervision of subordinates' work, detailed structuring of tasks, and maximum application of the division of labour. Employee-centred leadership, in contrast, emphasised the human and social aspects of subordinates' jobs. Here, employees are given widely defined tasks and left to complete them in their own ways. Workers are allowed discretion in how they achieve predetermined goals. Likert collected data on productivity, absenteeism, staff turnover, output quality and other efficiency indicators in several industrial and commercial organisations, concluding that employee-centred leadership was generally more efficient. Hence, work group supervisors should be trained in employee-centred leadership styles.

Effective supervisors, Likert found, do not practise close supervision, but expect high levels of performance from subordinates as a matter of course. They spend much time getting to know their workers and discussing projects with them. The best supervisors were those adopting a participative approach! There are, of course, problems associated with interpreting the results of such investigations. Frequently, workers and managers alter their behaviour when they know they are being observed. Also, leadership effectiveness is always difficult to measure because the consequences of managers adopting particular styles often depend as much on the quality of subordinates as on chosen leadership styles.

'Contingency' approaches to leadership argue that no one leadership style can ever be effective in all circumstances. Each approach has its strengths and weaknesses, and different styles should be applied depending on the situation. Leaders, contingency theorists argue, must be prepared to adjust their behaviour as circumstances change. Autocratic styles are appropriate when quick and/or unpopular decisions are needed, but the benefits of participation (use of subordinates' expert knowledge, higher morale, exercise of workers' initiative) are lost. Democratic approaches stimulate subordinates' motivation and sense of involvement; there is consensus on what should be done and general commitment to decisions reached, yet decisions might fail through the lack of experience and expert knowledge of those contributing to them. Moreover, participative decision taking procedures may be long-winded and inefficient. Thus, different work situations call for different leadership styles. A relaxed, democratic approach is appropriate in some circumstances; autocratic styles in others.

FE Fiedler sought to identify factors that determine the nature of situations.[1] Three such factors were found to be especially important:

- relationships between the leader and the group; in particular the degree of confidence of the group in the leader's abilities
- the nature of the tasks undertaken by subordinates: whether the tasks are easy or difficult, routine or varied
- how much authority is vested in the leader.

Fiedler described two contrasting leadership styles: people orientated (associated with considerate, understanding, treatment of subordinates) and task orientated — where the leader is directive and authoritarian.

Each style, he argued, is relevant to particular situations. People orientated leadership is useful, Fiedler concluded, where the work done by subordinates is liked even if the leader is disliked. If the work is disliked and the leader is unpopular, a more authoritarian manner may be appropriate.

Contingency theorists argue that management's role is to match leaders and situations and, to some extent, control situations. For example, people of similar backgrounds can be allocated to the same work groups so that a relatively homogeneous departmental workforce can be formed. Jobs can be made less varied and more precise, or extended to allow workers greater discretion in how they complete their work. Supervisors exhibiting certain leadership styles should be allocated to groups most likely to respond favourably to them. Leaders should change their styles to correspond with the demands of various situations: a leader might be permissive with one group; authoritarian with another. Leaders should be willing and able to use a variety of leadership styles, depending on the characteristics of subordinates, the nature of their work, and the surrounding environment.

Activity

The contingency approach seems to be common sense. To what extent do you adapt your leadership style to meet the needs of the situation?

Most of us like to think that we are adaptable and not set in our ways. However, if we do adapt our style, this may confuse subordinates. Evidence shows that, while subordinates might prefer a more participative, open leadership style, what they value above all is consistency.

An interesting attempt to relate autocratic and permissive management styles was the work of Robert Blake and Jane Mouton who designed a 'managerial grid' illustrating contrasting degrees of concern for human relations and for efficiency.[2] The grid is a taxonomy of management styles classified according to the manager's interest in subordinates as people in comparison with his or her concern for production. Each concern is rated on a scale from one to nine so that a '9,9' manager for example is one who possesses both a very high concern for people and a high concern for production. A '1,9' manager, with low concern for production but great emphasis on human relations, pays careful attention to subordinates' human needs, but exerts little effort to ensure that work is actually done. Such a manager is likeable, enjoys satisfactory relations with subordinates and generates a friendly atmosphere in his or her department. The '9,1' manager arranges work as efficiently as possible, with scant regard for subordinates' feelings. Other potential combinations are '1,1' managers, who make little effort to get work done or develop close personal relationships, and '5,5' managers who balance task performance with human relations considerations. Best of all is the '9,9' manager who achieves high production from committed, satisfied subordinates.

The question, 'What makes a good leader?' has no simple answer. Personal qualities, the leader's behaviour and the situation confronted might, it seems, affect performance. Thus, you need to experiment with a variety of styles and select whichever works best for you; though I suspect you will find the participative approach to be the most productive. Recognise that there need not be any 'best' style — that some people prefer being told what to do rather than being consulted and expected to participate in taking decisions. 'Task' centred leadership, properly applied, can be extremely effective. You take the initiative in developing activities, in defining problems and suggesting solutions — you propose new ways of doing things rather than reacting to events. You consciously seek out information and ideas, and issue instructions based on the facts you discover — seeking always to *help* your subordinates in their work. You clarify issues, put things together, and generally become the centre of the team.

Accept equally, however, that assertive approaches can degenerate to dominance and unpleasant aggression and that the application of participative styles to *trivial* issues while simultaneously refusing consultation on *major* decisions may be bitterly resented by employees. Explain your mode of behaviour to subordinates, and be prepared to justify your chosen style. If you feel an autocratic manner is appropriate, then tell your staff why you believe this to be so — there must be a reason for your choice and if you are unhappy about revealing what the reason is you should seriously reconsider the propriety of your motives. Listen sympathetically to subordinates' suggestions, (regardless of your adopted style) and keep the staff fully informed of what you expect them to do.

Activity

How is your effectiveness as a leader measured? What should it be based on?

This is a very difficult question. The effectiveness of a leader is often based on the performance of his/her subordinates and their ability to meet targets set. Particularly in the short term, the leader who achieves results through fear and intimidation may be viewed as effective. It is only in the long term, when staff turnover figures are measured, or transfer requests totalled, that his/her methods may be questioned.

At the other extreme, where the leader is seen as 'one of the boys' and is liked by everyone, this has to be set against the output of the group. Poor performance by the group cannot be offset by the popularity of the leader.

Effective leadership frequently depends on the efficiency (or otherwise) of departmental communications and on the design of working environments. Examine, therefore, the efficiency of your management by objectives system, briefing sessions, job enlargement and enrichment schemes and work planning procedures. Ensure that you are readily accessible to subordinates, that you know something about their backgrounds and aspirations and that all your subordinates' contributions are properly recognised.

At its best, 'people' rather than task centred behaviour brings subordinates together through involving them closely in all the work of the team. Here, you concentrate on encouraging staff to initiate activity and suggest new ideas. You listen, empathise, explore differences of opinion, inspire friendliness and encourage the acceptance of other people's views. You *suggest* rather than impose solutions to problems, and accept compromises when subordinates disagree with your opinions.

Often, it is easier to appreciate the significance of an idea if you know where it originated, the reason for its existence and the elements of opposing views. Leadership theories are derivatives of more general approaches to management studies. The development of various 'schools of thought' in management is briefly outlined in the next section.

A brief history of management thought

Management theory derives largely from the work of a small number of analysts and practitioners active during the early part of the twentieth century (the study of management as an academic discipline is relatively new). The contributions of the major writers are summarised below, in roughly the order in which they appeared.

Activity

The remainder of the chapter is devoted to management theories. As you read through, you will find many of the ideas contradictory and therefore confusing. You do not have to accept any of the ideas put forward, but try to keep an open mind.

You may find it useful to take a sheet of paper and draw a thumbnail sketch of each theory for subsequent comparison.

FW Taylor (1856–1915) and the scientific school

FW Taylor qualified as an engineer in 1883 while working for the Midvale Steel Company in the US. Taylor developed what came to be known as the 'scientific' approach to management, which he expounded in two books: *Shop Management*, published in 1906 and *The Principles of Scientific Management*, published in 1911. His philosophy was simple: workers' were motivated (he believed) by the prospect of high material reward, so that provided workers' wages were closely linked to the volumes of their outputs and provided working methods were designed to maximise production, then employees would work as hard as they possibly could and would produce good quality output. There were three basic principles to scientific management.

- Workers should be set relatively high targets to stretch them to their maximum capacities. Daily workloads should be specified by management following detailed analysis of jobs and the most efficient ways in which they would be done.
- Wherever possible, work should be completed under 'standard conditions' involving the most efficient working methods. Working environments should be carefully controlled and the division of labour applied to its maximum extent. Each operative was thus responsible for just a small number of tasks. Constant repetition of operations developed speed, skill and, consequently, high volumes of good quality production. No time should be wasted in fetching raw materials, arranging tools, or transporting finished work. Duplication of effort was to be avoided.
- Pay should be directly related to productivity, hence stimulating effort and encouraging cooperation with management. Taylor even suggested the use of differential payment schemes in which employees who exceeded target performance would receive large bonuses whereas workers falling below target would incur significant wage cuts.

The practical application of these principles required the measurement and analysis of work, including study and timing of physical movements. Once a job had been evaluated, the type of person most likely to succeed in its execution could be identified. Workers' training needs were defined through systematic investigation of the skills necessary for particular types of work.

According to Taylor, management should plan and direct all the employees' efforts, leaving little discretion for individual control over working methods. Job specifications should be clear, simple and distinct; the fewer functions an individual was required to perform the better. The organisation should be controlled through application of the 'principle of exception' whereby subordinates would submit to their superiors only brief, condensed, reports on normal operations, but extensive reports on deviations from past average performance or targets set by higher management. Once established, standards would be monitored by picking out significant divergences from predetermined norms. Exceptionally good or bad results would be analysed in depth and explanations offered, but reasonable deviations from normal performance would not be questioned.

Taylor was not popular with either workers or managerial colleagues. Indeed, towards the end of his life he described his earlier time and motion activities in the following words:[4]

> I was a young man in years but I give you my word I was a great deal older than I am now, what with the worry, meanness, and contemptibleness of the whole darn thing. It's a horrid life for any man to live not being able to look any workman in the face without seeing hostility there, and a feeling that every man around you is your virtual enemy.

Labour unions also were unimpressed by Taylor's new methods and the introduction of scientific management techniques provoked widespread opposition from organised labour. Unemployment often results from increased industrial efficiency as fewer people are needed to produce a given amount of goods. This, together with the loss of individual control over working practices and procedures that the scientific approach implies, aroused distrust, fear and antagonism amongst workers. The division of labour creates boredom for those who perform routine tasks. Constant repetition of simple movements dehumanises work: individuals become appendages of the machines they operate. In the longer term, moreover, excessive application of the division of labour could alienate workers to the extent that less is produced than otherwise would be the case. Note also that scientific management focused its attention on efficiency on the factory-floor rather than at higher levels within organisations. The existing social environment was assumed constant, and was accepted without question. The scientific school did not question the ethics of private enterprise, or consider the influences on productivity that differing cultural or political regimes might exert.

Contemporaries and followers of Taylor extended and developed the scientific approach. HL Gantt for example pioneered the use of statistical production control. He devised performance charts for operatives, machines and processes

---

Self-check

Identify the three basic principles of scientific management.

Answer

— management should set targets for workers to reach
— management identifies the most efficient method of work and ensures that workers comply
— pay is linked to productivity, thus rewarding those who work efficiently and achieve targets.

---

allowing simultaneous comparison of several activities in terms of costs, idle time, stoppages, etc. Frank B Gilbreth investigated the principles of human body motion in work situations. Following an initial study of the body movements required for bricklaying, Gilbreth extended his analysis to other types of work until, eventually, he had compiled a complete system for the measurement and classification of all the basic human body motions used at work.

Advocates of scientific management recognised the importance of a co-operative workforce. Willingness to accept scientific principles would, they believed, automatically emerge, since employees were assumed to be motivated by the overwhelming desire for economic reward. Thus, any device for increasing efficiency, and hence wages, would be accepted.

Henri Fayol (1841–1925)

Fayol was a French mining engineer who wrote extensively on management topics. His most influential work was a short book, *General and Industrial Management*, which first appeared in France in 1916. He believed in the universality of certain principles of administration. Organisations, he argued, were involved in five types of 'activity': technical, commercial, security, finance and accounting, and management. The latter — management — could be split into five broad areas: planning and forecasting, organisation, command, coordination and control. Forecasting and planning meant looking into the future and deciding today what shall be done in the future depending on the occurrence of certain events. *Organisation* was the process of dividing work into units and allocating these to people and departments. *Command* involved issuing instructions to ensure that targets were met. *Coordination* meant the unification of effort, while *control* required setting targets, monitoring activity to ensure that targets were met and taking remedial action to deal with divergences of actual from target performance.

Unlike FW Taylor, Fayol was less interested in questions of day to day operations than in the broad structure of administration. The fundamental principles of administration — applicable, he suggested, to any form of organisation — were as follows:

- specialisation and the division of labour
- unity of command (i.e., one person one boss)
- linkage of authority and responsibility, so that the occupant of a post possesses the authority needed to carry its responsibilities
- a fair internal disciplinary system
- the setting of objectives throughout the organisation, and the centralisation of plans to provide a 'unity of direction' for the entire firm
- use of organisation charts and job descriptions
- creation of stable work groups and job security for personnel.

Collectively, the efforts of Henri Fayol, FW Taylor and his followers, and Max Weber (1864–1920, see chapter 2) are referred to as the 'classical school'. This emphasises formal rules, specialisation, clear division of responsibilities, and the achievement of high efficiency through the analysis of work. It attaches relatively little importance to the human and social needs of the people who operate the organisation.

Self-check

Which writers belong to the classical school? How much importance does this school attach to human and social needs of workers?

Answer

Fayol, Taylor, Gantt, Gilbreth and Weber.

Little importance is attached to the human and social needs of workers. The emphasis is on efficiency through formal rules, clear structure and methods of work derived from scientific study.

The work of G Elton Mayo (1880–1949)

Through concentrating on mercenary, economic, aspects of human nature the scientific school tended to ignore the social and psychological needs of employees. Yet, these psycho-sociological factors exert powerful influences on behaviour. One of the first theorists openly to question the validity of the scientific approach was Elton Mayo, an Australian-born American sociologist who largely founded the 'human relations' school. Mayo and his associates conducted an extensive study of management practice at a plant (known as the 'Hawthorne' plant) of the Western Electric Company in Chicago, USA, between the years of 1927 and 1932. Initially, Mayo was a disciple of FW Taylor and was attracted to the proposition that efficiency can be increased simply by altering the physical circumstances of work. Accordingly, when asked by Western Electric to suggest how performance at the Hawthorne plant might be improved he sought to measure the effects of changes in physical working conditions which, according to the scientific management school, should cause significant variations in productivity. Lighting, heating, noise levels etc were altered and resulting output changes noted. In fact, production altered counter-intuitively as physical conditions were varied. Output increased *whenever* conditions were changed, even if the alteration made conditions worse! Workers involved knew they were being observed. This knowledge enhanced their self-esteem, and the fact that they were the subject of experiments seemed to encourage cooperative behaviour. It emerged, moreover, that social relationships exerted strong influences on production levels. The work groups under observation became interested in the experiments and consequently group morale and productivity increased. Physical conditions such as lighting and heating were relatively unimportant compared to inter-personal relationships within groups and relations between groups and their supervisors. A major finding, and a damaging one from the viewpoint of the scientific school, was that wages were not the dominant motivator for these employees. Workers' actual behaviour depended on norms and standards established through contacts with other people within and beyond the working group.

Many researchers have attempted to repeat the Hawthorne experiments, with varied results. Mayo has been criticised for drawing sweeping conclusions from small sample observations, for ignoring wider political and social influences beyond the factory on work group behaviour, and for ignoring the potential effects of unionisation (the Western Electric Company was waging an anti-union campaign and would not recognise unions at the time of the study). Nevertheless, the Hawthorne studies have been enormously influential, and work by Mayo's followers has established the 'human relations approach' as a major school of management thought.

Self-check

What conclusions did Mayo draw from observations during the Hawthorne experiments?

Answer
Whatever the working conditions, workers maintained and even increased levels of output. The reasons were two-fold; firstly the workers felt important as they were part of an experiment and wanted to do well, secondly the group set its own norms and standards of behaviour.

If you read on, you will find outlined in the text the basic ideas put forward by the human relations school.

The fundamental propositions of the human relations approach are as follows:

- the amount of work a person does depends not so much on physical strength or dexterity, or even on the physical conditions in which tasks are performed; rather it depends on the social conditions surrounding the work
- non-economic rewards can motivate workers more than high wages; feelings of happiness and security often result from factors independent of pay
- specialisation and the division of labour are not necessarily efficient. Giving workers a wide variety of tasks, some of which require the exercise of initiative and discretion, can stimulate interest to the point where productivity increases
- individuals perceive themselves as members of groups. Norms of behaviour emanate from standards set by groups to which workers belong, and not from standards imposed by management.

Douglas McGregor (1906–1964)

A particularly important contribution to the development of the human relations approach was the work of D McGregor who examined the implications of scientific management's interpretation of human nature.[5] McGregor's work is commonly referred to as theory X and theory Y.

Theory X and theory Y

In his 1945 text, *The Social Problems of an Industrial Society*,[6] Elton Mayo attacked the assumptions about human nature held by the classical school. These assumptions (which Mayo attributed — perhaps unfairly — to the English economist David Ricardo) were intertwined with notions of the survival of the fittest, laissez-faire, and the fundamental selfishness of man. Mayo describes what he considers to be the main postulates of these assumptions as follows:

(a) Natural society consists of a horde of unorganised individuals.

(b) Every individual acts in a manner calculated to secure that person's self-preservation or self-interest.

(c) Every individual thinks logically, to the best of his or her ability, in the service of this aim.

This assault on the fundamental *assumptions* of scientific management was developed by Douglas McGregor who outlined two alternative sets of assumptions about attitudes towards work. Theory X assumptions were those which (according to McGregor) autocratic managers were likely to adopt. An autocratic manager might honestly believe that the average person dislikes work and must therefore be coerced, directed and threatened with sanctions. Other theory X assumptions are that:

- people will avoid work if they can, so that inducements, sanctions, and close supervision are necessary to stimulate effort
- workers are naturally reluctant to assume responsibility, preferring the security of control by others
- people are happier with clearly defined tasks than broadly defined objectives.

In opposition to theory X McGregor recommended the adoption of an alternative set of assumptions about human nature. These he referred to as theory Y, the major propositions of which are as follows:

- workers normally devote as much effort to their work as to their home and recreational activities. Individuals will work hard without coercion
- generally, employees can be relied upon to exercise self-direction and self-control
- people seek rather than avoid responsibility
- industrial society constrains the realisation of individual creative potential. Such potential exists in most people, it has only to be extricated and developed.

Activity

You have just studied McGregor's two sets of assumptions about attitudes to work. Which view do you agree with, theory X or Y?

While you may not be able wholeheartedly to accept either view, you must feel more drawn to one or the other. Clearly, your opinion, as a leader, on why people work, will influence your attitude towards them and your style of leadership.

The modern management trend is to favour theory Y as you will see from McGregor's comments.

McGregor condemned the Theory X suppositions that the average employee will not work hard unless coerced into doing so and that workers require continuous supervision and detailed specification of tasks. Work, he argues, is natural to the human species, and those who perform work will normally devote their full attention, effort and interest to its completion. Thus, management's primary concern should be to harness the innate energy and willingness to cooperate of the workforce — managers do not have to coerce and threaten workers to make them work hard; employees are capable of self-control.

To the extent that theory Y assumptions are valid, organisations should be designed to accommodate social and human needs. They should encourage personal initiative and release creative potential. Rigid organisational forms are said to inhibit the innate enthusiasm of junior managerial staff, hence reducing efficiency. Advocates of theory Y recommend participative management. Targets jointly determined by subordinate and superior will be more readily accepted than targets that are arbitrarily imposed. Of course, problems regarding quantification of objectives will occur as will disagreements about what represents a reasonable objective, but the full knowledge, skills and experiences of lower managers will be utilised in decision taking processes and those involved will feel direct personal responsibility for achieving objectives they helped to set.

Contingency theory and the systems approach

Chester I Barnard (1886–1961) noted in the 1930s that organisations possess powerful informal systems that run in parallel with official structures.[7] An organisation is, he suggested, a cooperative system; there is upward as well as downward communication and unofficial leaders emerge — the organisation is a *system* consisting of several networks of individuals interacting together and with the environment.

Many writers have developed the theme of the organisation as a system dependent on interrelations between its component parts and with the outside world. Businesses, for instance, exist in 'open' systems. They have relations with customers, suppliers, neighbours and local and national governments and the usefulness of a particular management style could be affected by these relationships. There are, for example, laws that govern the conduct of industrial relations between firms and employees; limited liability companies are required to apply certain rules regarding rights and duties of shareholders; and there are laws to protect customers from untruthful advertisements.

The systems approach enables changes in environmental conditions and their effects on management to be analysed methodically. An example of a systems factor might be an alteration in the people to whom an organisation is accountable — the structure and management style of a firm which must account for its actions to just one or two people will probably differ from the approach adopted by a firm that is accountable to a large number of shareholders or to the government. Managements which are required to justify their actions to employees will have different attitudes to those which are not.

Systems theory emphasises the need for those in control of a system to define its boundaries clearly. Are, for example, a firm's customers to be considered an integral part of the organisation, or does the system end at the point of sale? Often, a system can be accurately described through specifying where its boundaries lie and many insights into how a particular system operates can be obtained by analysing what happens there.

The contingency approach emphasises the need for flexibility in organisational design and style of leadership. It asserts the impossibility of generalising about appropriate management behaviour for differing situations. Each set of circumstances is unique. For example, a military exercise might require the coercion of large numbers of unwilling soldiers to perform dangerous, unpopular tasks. A management style relevant to this situation will not be the same as one suitable for managing a business firm and circumstances within particular organisations vary between departments over time. The contingency approach is diagnostic rather than prescriptive, suggesting that management's role is to identify characteristics which define situations and then apply management techniques appropriate to specific circumstances. The obvious problem is the vast range of variables — environmental, social, physical, economic, legal, technical, industrial — potentially relevant to each situation. Note that although feelings of contentment, happiness and job satisfaction do improve workers' performances, not all working environments can be made satisfying or even interesting for the staff involved. Some work is necessarily unpleasant but still has to be done. It might be simply impossible to create pleasant working environments or adjust conditions to meet the social needs of employees. In this case, financial reward is probably the key motivator and a contingency theorist would recommend payments systems which directly relate wages and effort as would an advocate of the scientific management school.

Summary

You have had a chance to study the role/s of management within an organisation and the various styles that a leader might adopt in performing his/her role.

Now is the time to have a look at the sheets you have drawn up as part of the activities prescribed in the chapter, and review the theories outlined.

It is difficult to analyse your own role within an organisation and identify the style of leadership you favour, but you will find it a worthwhile exercise. Ask some of your subordinates what kind of leader you are and what approach you use when dealing with them. You may be surprised to discover that their perception of you is very different from your own. What are your shortcomings and how can you overcome them?

Notes

1 Fiedler, FE, *A Theory of Leadership Effectiveness*, McGraw-Hill, New York, 1967.
2 Blake, RR and Mouton, J, *The Management Grid*, Gulf Publishing, Houston, Texas, 1964.
3 Likert, R, *New Patterns of Management*, McGraw-Hill, New York, 1961.
4 Quoted in Brown, JAC, *The Social Psychology of Industry*, p 14, Pelican, 1954.
5 McGregor, D, *The Human Side of Enterprise*, McGraw-Hill, New York, 1960.
6 Mayo, E, *The Social Problems of an Industrial Society*, Harvard University Press, Boston, 1945.
7 Barnard, C, *Functions of the Executive*, Harvard University Press, Cambridge, Mass, 1938.

5
Motivation

Objectives

At the end of this chapter you will be able to:

- analyse the reasons why people work and recognise the implications for motivation and performance in the workplace
- recognise the symptoms of lack of motivation in staff
- apply the principles of good job design to improve staff motivation

Employees are motivated in part by the need to earn a living and partly by human needs for job satisfaction, security of tenure, the respect of colleagues and so on. The organisation's reward system (pay, fringe benefits, job security, promotion opportunities, etc) may be applied to the first motive and job design to the latter. Much research has sought to discover the sources of motivation at work, but no definitive conclusions have emerged — it seems that many factors motivate individuals. Central to all theories of motivation is the concept of *need*, and how people seek to justify their perceived requirements.

Attitudes towards work

Controversy surrounds the question whether there exists in humans a natural instinct to work. An instinct is innate, it is born within the person and does not have to be learned. Some theorists suggest that work is a natural activity and that left to themselves workers will normally work hard. Others assume that employees dislike work, will avoid it wherever possible and thus will require close and constant supervision.

Activity

List as many reasons as you can why people work and what needs are satisfied through work.

Set your list on one side and we will refer to it again at the end of the chapter.

In modern industrialised societies most people have to work whether they like it or not. Work provides income, social status and a means whereby individuals become involved with society. Work, usually, is a social activity, few people work entirely alone. The fact that work brings people into contact with others is itself a powerful motivator in making them want to work. Not only does unemployment cause reductions in workers' incomes but it also severs many of their links with society. Thus, social factors (as well as pay) are relevant to the incentive to work. Note particularly how physical working conditions are not necessarily related to workers' morale.

Few people would claim to have found the perfect job; all jobs involve some routine work or unenjoyable activities. Monotonous, uncreative work does however cause special difficulties, including the following.

Boredom

Boredom may result from continuous repetition of a simple task, or from the social environment in which tasks are undertaken. A task might be interesting, but the worker still feel bored if he or she must complete it in isolation. Equally, jobs can be trivial and repetitious, yet not create boredom because workers are able to communicate pleasurably with others. Workers who perform complex tasks typically become absorbed by them and are not bored.

Frustration

Workers experience frustration when they are prevented from exercising control over their work and are not able to achieve their (self-defined) objectives. Frustration can be caused by the lack of control over working methods or the speed of production, by having to do work perceived as meaningless, through not being involved in decision making or through workers not feeling that their grievances have been properly heard. A worker may react to frustration positively, by attempting to overcome the problem that caused the obstruction, or negatively. Examples of negative reactions are aggression (quarrels with colleagues, hostility towards management), apathy (lateness, absenteeism), unwillingness to assume responsibility, poor quality work, high propensities to have accidents and high rates of labour turnover.

Alienation

This is the feeling that work is not a relevant or important part of one's life; that one does not really belong to the work community. It is associated with feelings of discontent, isolation and futility. Alienated workers perceive themselves as powerless and dominated. Work becomes simply a means to achieve material ends. Great unhappiness can result from alienation, indeed, the mental or physical health of the employee can suffer. Alienation may result from lack of contact with other workers and/or with management, from authoritarian or paternalistic management styles or simply through the boredom of routine work. Its consequences are numerous: poor quality output, absenteeism, resistance to change, industrial disputes, deteriorating interpersonal relationships etc.

People usually work better when they feel they have a personal stake in the success of their activities — success not necessarily measured in financial terms. Money is obviously important, but many other factors are involved: staff might accept that they are well paid, yet still be dissatisfied with their jobs. Consider, for example, the highly-paid executive for whom a wage rise will mostly disappear in tax, or the person who automatically hands over the bulk of his or her earnings to someone else (a husband, wife or parent for instance), or the employee who already possesses a large private income. Proper pay and decent working conditions are obviously the foundations that underlie good relations between workers and the firm but thereafter other factors come to the fore. In particular, it seems that fair and equal treatment of workers greatly motivate employees.

Nevertheless, the importance of money as a motivator should not be underestimated, although the degree of motivation it provides varies from person to person. The point is that monetary wage increases can be used for many purposes: to buy goods and services, to change lifestyle, support a leisure activity, etc. Also a pay rise is an explicit recognition of a person's occupational competence: pay rises awarded for excellent performance can greatly increase a worker's commitment and general morale. This itself can be a motivating factor. Comparison of a person's wages with the wages of others enables the individual to relate his or her job to other jobs both within the organisation and externally. There can be no doubt that relations with colleagues, pride in the quality of one's work, group cohesion, etc, are major motivators; but wage increases remain a primary factor.

Self-check

What factors might indicate a lack of job satisfaction on the part of your staff?

Answer

As a general rule of thumb, unacceptable behaviour signifies that all may not be well.

Poor job performance — in terms of quality, quantity or both
High absenteeism
High labour turnover
Frequent staff disputes and squabbles over minor matters.

The nature of work

Certain types of work provide employees with opportunities for creativity and the exercise of initiative (managerial work for example) and those who undertake such work typically derive great satisfaction from its completion. For others, however, work can be a drudge, neither enjoyable not satisfying, just something that has to be done. The latter situation is particularly unfortunate in situations where individuals are in jobs which are clearly unsuited to their abilities, aptitudes and perspectives. To the extent that people are well adjusted to their jobs, their morale, effort and efficiency is enhanced.

Individual differences

Each person enters the labour force possessing a particular stock of attributes. People have differing levels of ability, differing personalities, interests and temperaments. Individuals are dissimilar in their physical appearance, voice and manner. Certain people seem to possess natural aptitudes for particular tasks (those requiring manual dexterity or mental arithmetic for example) and individual personalities are unique — some people are introverted, others extrovert, some are sociable, others happiest when working alone.

Activity

Analyse your own attitude to work. Do you work to live or live to work? What aspects of work do you enjoy and what aspects do you dislike?

This is not an easy task but if you can understand your own attitudes, it may help you to appreciate the attitudes of your staff. We are all individuals, with our own needs and objectives, but at work we tend to be treated as part of a group.

Work requires social behaviour — cooperation, supervision, interpersonal bargaining, assessment and appraisal of others. Thus, social skills are needed to cope at work. From an early age children are socialised into the culture of work. They are prepared for the work experience through vocational education, careers guidance, school-to-work transition programmes, work induction and special training schemes. Whether the school-leaver eagerly looks forward to work as an exciting challenge or approaches work with fear and trepidation will depend fundamentally on attitudes towards and perceptions of work within the society in which the school-leaver has been brought up.

People usually first learn about work through hearing their parents' conversations about their jobs and through observing parents' going to and returning from places of work. Young children do not work as such, but their play often reflects themes derived from their parents' occupations. As they grow up they do increasing amounts of school work. They have no experience of specific types of occupation, yet attitudes consistent with occupational success are inculcated in them at school.

Scholastic achievement is rewarded and success in competitive sports encouraged. Parents and teachers constantly exhort young people to do well in work-related activities and aspects of personality specifically relevant to occupational success (intelligence, initiative, ability to concentrate for long periods) are systematically developed. Discipline patterns in schools, moreover, are often justified against their value in training young people to fit into patterns of supervision and authority at work.

During these formative years individuals acquire self-identities which they carry into work. An individual's self-identity (or self-image) consists of a whole set of perceptions that a person has about him or her self. Such perceptions derive from individual experiences and personalities and offer a way of interpreting an individual's social role. Teenagers, for example, typically perceive their role as different to those of the middle-aged or retired and behave in accordance with the perceived requirements of that role (few old age pensioners ride motor cycles for instance, while teenagers rarely eat in restaurants frequented mostly by the middle aged). The way in which individuals perceive their social roles usually alters with respect to age, family circumstances and occupation. People see themselves differently as they get older, wealthier and as they are promoted at work. They act differently and expect others to alter their behaviour towards them.

The importance of self-image

Self-image is important for understanding attitudes towards work because the ideas people hold about themselves affect their behaviour. Individuals tend to act in ways that conform to their self-identities. Note however how self-perceptions can be entirely wrong. Often we view our own attributes and abilities in unreasonably favourable ways. Note also how easy it is for a person to confuse occupational status with genuine ability: promotion to a high ranking job for example does not necessarily mean that a person is intellectually superior to those who were passed over for promotion.

Self-image is important too for helping individuals choose particular lines of work. In selecting an occupation, adolescents are guided by the advice they receive from teachers and careers officers and by parental role models. Additionally, youngsters are likely to be attracted by jobs associated with characteristics which they perceive themselves to possess. A boy, for example, who sees himself as a gregarious type will probably not want a job that involves spending long periods alone. It follows that different types of work might be favoured at different stages of a person's life depending on age, family circumstances etc because perceptions alter over time. A 15 year-old looks at life quite differently to someone who is 25, married with children and paying a mortgage.

Self-image and occupation are to some extent interdependent. Many factors contribute to a final choice of job: availability, the nature of local industry, the example of older people and individual personality. Having taken a job, the employee might then begin to adopt outlooks and patterns of behaviour associated with that type of work. Newcomers to organisations often copy the behaviour of existing members and continued exposure to organisational norms will lead them to assimilate the norms and attitudes of the organisations to which they belong. Professionals similarly construct self-identities, but often identify more closely with the profession itself than with a particular firm. Usually, a professionally qualified person wants a career — a logically planned series of increasingly responsible jobs — rather than a single post. Some professionals prefer to change firms frequently, relying on their professional expertise, abilities, and motivation to secure progressively senior posts; others choose to spend most of their careers in one large organisation which offers steady progression towards a senior management job.

Self-check

What is self-image and how does it influence one's attitude to work?

Answer

Self-image is an individual's perception of him/herself and will influence how he/she acts in any given situation. It frequently influences the choice of career as the individual will select the job which most closely matches the characteristics they perceive themselves as possessing.

Self-image often changes over time as one grows older. Having chosen a career, individuals may adopt the behaviour and attitudes of those around them.

As individuals are promoted they acquire new images of themselves. The self-identity of a supervisor for example is usually quite different to that of a middle management line executive, who in turn will possess a self-image different to that held by a person occupying a very senior post. Following promotion, managers will mix with people whose attitudes might contrast with those previously encountered, so that adjustments in attitude, behaviour and, ultimately, self-perception are required. Promotion brings a higher status, extra income and possibly a whole new way of life.

Managerial work

Activity

Define managerial work. What job titles do you associate with management?

Read on and compare your views with those in the text. Management is a broad term, covering a wide variety of tasks.

A managerial job comprises a whole series of characteristics including skill requirements, education, training and experience needed, physical requirements for the type of work involved, the degree of responsibility assumed and working conditions. Other requirements might include the abilities to plan, coordinate and control the work of others, to withstand stress and qualities of initiative, reliability and willingness to work as part of a team. To be good at management you must learn to work with other people. You will have superiors and subordinates, through whom you will achieve results. It might be possible to avoid extensive contact with other departments but this is undesirable. Senior management skills can be quite different to the skills acquired during early training: abilities to plan, coordinate and take strategic rather than operational decisions become paramount.

What is a manager?

Many categories of employee now call themselves manager: supervisors, professional advisors, consultants and those who are concerned more with physical resources than people. There are, nevertheless, common elements in most managerial jobs. Perhaps the most common denominator is the unpredictability and variability of managerial work. Management typically involves doing lots of fragmented jobs. It involves therefore communication with others and requires an ability to appreciate the significance of their work.

Henry Mintzberg pointed out[1] the contradictions that sometimes arise between managers' job specifications and the duties they actually perform. According to Mintzberg, the classical approach to management (see above) assigned to managers highly specific responsibilities — planning, organising, coordinating, and so on; whereas other approaches viewed the manager's role differently — as leadership, profit-maximisation, ensuring long run survival etc. Yet all management work, Mintzberg argued, has common elements, which he categorised under three headings: interpersonal, informational and decisional. In their interpersonal role, managers act as figureheads, leaders and coordinators. The informational role involves the collection, monitoring and transmission of information and the control of working groups. Decisional aspects of management work require individuals to initiate change, allocate resources, negotiate and handle disturbances. All managerial activity, Mintzberg commented, is characterised by pace, frequent interruption, variety, fragmentation of effort, the need for quick thinking and regular verbal communications with others.

Exactly *how* a manager undertakes such activities depends on the particular circumstances of the situation, on the manager's personality and the environments in which the manager and the organisation function. Management, argued Mintzberg, is an *art*, and as such, management skills can only be nurtured within individuals through self-analysis and appraisal, and through personal self-development.

Much controversy has surrounded the question whether management may be regarded as a bona fide profession. Without doubt, certain aspects of management have professional characteristics — they are intellectually demanding, require the exercise of discretion and application of expert knowledge and mistakes and bad decisions lead to serious adverse consequences for the firm. Yet the substance of management is extremely diverse. Management is necessarily a generic subject involving a great variety of fragmented jobs — if there is a single common denominator in managerial work it is the variability and unpredictability of tasks!

Self-check

How did Mintzberg categorise management work?

Answer

Interpersonal: figurehead, leader, co-ordinator

Informational: collection, monitoring and transmission of information, control of work groups

Decisional: allocation of resources, negotiations, coping with change

He viewed management as an art, where the skills needed have to be developed over time.

To qualify for true professional status, three conditions must apply. Firstly, professional activities should be based on an established and systematic body of knowledge, the acquisition of which requires several years of substantial intellectual training. Secondly, entry to the profession should be restricted to persons possessing certain predetermined qualifications and experience. Thirdly, carefully specified ethical (professional) standards should be maintained and codes of practice followed.

Management does not satisfy these criteria. No formal qualifications are needed to become a manager. Indeed many successful managers (especially entrepreneurs) have received only rudimentary academic qualifications. No generally accepted norms of management conduct exist (other than those imposed by government via legislation or regulatory bodies); and there are no uniform management principles to which managers are forced to adhere. Nevertheless, there is a strong case for treating management as if it were a profession. Modern managers must be encouraged to take a professional pride in the quality of their output — efficient and socially responsible management should come to be viewed as an end in itself and not just a means for earning a living.

Job design

Job design is the process of deciding which tasks and responsibilities shall be undertaken by particular employees and the methods, systems and procedures for completing work. It concerns patterns of accountability and authority, spans of control and interpersonal relations between colleagues. The purpose of job design is to stimulate the interest and involvement of the worker, thus motivating the worker to greater efforts. Jobs may be *enlarged* or *enriched*.

Job enlargement means increasing the scope of a job through extending the range of its duties and responsibilities. This contradicts the principle of specialisation and division of labour whereby work is divided into small units, each of which is performed repetitively by an individual worker. The boredom and alienation caused by the division of labour can actually cause efficiency to fall, thus, job enlargement seeks to motivate workers through reversing the process of specialisation.

Job enrichment involves the allocation of more interesting, challenging and perhaps difficult duties to workers in order to stimulate their sense of participation and concern for the achievement of objectives. Extra decision-making authority may be assigned to workers or they might be given duties requiring higher skill levels or be required to have greater contact with customers and/or suppliers. Equally, existing single tasks might be combined into a composite whole or workers might be made responsible for controlling the quality of their output, or be allowed greater discretion over how they achieve objectives. It is essential to involve trade union or other workers' representatives from the very outset of any attempt to enrich jobs. Trade unions are naturally suspicious that in enriching jobs management seeks only to extract from workers more work for the same amount of pay.

The term job *extension* is used to embrace both enlargement and enrichment. Its underlying philosophy is, quite simply, that the wider the variety of tasks undertaken the more the worker realises the significance of the job in the wider organisation and the happier and more productive the worker will become. Of course, some jobs are more easily extended than others. Assembly lines in automated factories offer few opportunities for interesting work. In this case, higher pay and/or greater worker participation could be primary motivators. Note also that not everybody wants to assume extra responsibility. In situations where job enlargement is not possible, an alternative is to put workers through sequences of different jobs. Each job is boring, but monotony is relieved through regular job rotation. Thus, workers experience many jobs at different stages in the production process, even though the division of labour has been fully applied. Moreover, employee absences can then be covered from an existing pool of trained, experienced personnel.

To initiate a job design exercise you must first analyse the work that needs to be done using existing job descriptions and data from previous work study programmes. You should know which jobs are least interesting to the people who do them (and why) and what steps are necessary to make these jobs more interesting. Thus, you should interview subordinates individually (performance appraisal discussions offer convenient opportunities for this), confidentially and sympathetically in order to get the *feel* of their jobs. Unfortunately, people often exaggerate the difficulties and problems associated with their work, so you must pin interviewees down when describing their jobs; do not accept vague statements about tasks and responsibilities.

Self-check

What are the benefits to be derived from specialisation? How would you argue in favour of job enlargement over specialisation?

Answer
Benefits include — shortened training period, increased productivity and efficiency, lower labour costs as less skilled labour can be used.

Job enlargement gives an individual more duties and responsibilities. Studies have found that specialisation can lead to monotonous jobs, to the extent that the benefits of higher efficiency and productivity are not achieved.

Having described subordinates' jobs, list the *interesting* duties — those which carry responsibility and which involve planning and self-control — associated with each position. Then specify exactly the changes necessary to make particularly boring jobs more interesting, eg the regrouping of activities (taking some interesting work away from certain individuals for reallocation to others), allowing workers to alter the pace or methods of their work or allocating broad rather than specific objectives. Participation in the setting of targets can also enrich employees' work, especially if the workers are encouraged to contribute completely new ideas.

Satisfied staff are easy to supervise, they are productive, cooperative and easy to please. Look critically at subordinates' physical working conditions. Can they be improved? Can you enhance the perceived status of subordinates, say by giving each of their jobs an impressive sounding title? Possibly, you can improve subordinates' sense of job security through frequently complementing their standards of work and you might perhaps reduce the amount of supervision you apply by removing various controls (time sheets, rigid directives on working methods, standard layouts for equipment and materials, etc). Can the staff be brought into contact with final customers, or even other departments which utilise their work? Much satisfaction can be gained from observing the pleasure of a customer when he or she is presented with a high quality finished product. Try to make your staff feel important, praise them and be seen to take a personal interest in their work.

Empowerment and the quality of working life

Employees will normally be more productive if, rather than just tolerating their lives at work, they actually enjoy the work experience. Job design is one means for making employees' work more interesting. Other devices for improving the quality of working life (QWL) include involving people in workplace problem-solving and decision-making; the enhancement of environmental conditions; better communication within the organisation and employee participation in objective setting. Note particularly how an employee's feelings of being in control and of significantly contributing to an organisation's, development, can be greatly enhanced by 'empowering' that person to complete tasks and attain targets independently, without constantly having to refer back to management for permission to take certain actions. The employee is *trusted* to make sensible decisions. Hence, for example, salespeople might be empowered to offer special discounts to prospective customers, production operatives can be empowered to decide the speed of an assembly line, and work teams may be empowered to determine the extent and intensity of the use of robots within a section. Hopefully, empowerment will encourage personal initiative and creativity, ensure that decisions are made at the most suitable level, and help bond the worker to the firm.

Activity

Look closely at the jobs performed within your department. Identify those that are the most interesting and those that are the most boring. Can anything be done by means of job enlargement, job enrichment or job rotation to minimise the boredom factor?

You may well meet with a mixed reception if you try to implement any changes to working practices, but this should not be allowed to stand in the way of creating a more pleasant and satisfying working environment for the majority of staff.

Criticising staff

If you have to criticise a subordinate, criticise an action rather than the individual and always precede the criticism with a compliment regarding some other aspect of that person's work. You may find the following a useful procedure for presenting a criticism:

- choose a private place for the conversation, do not dramatise and never cause the subordinate to feel that you will publicise the criticism to others
- show that a problem has been caused by the subordinate's substandard performance. Ask for a comment on the situation
- suggest a means of overcoming the problem and together examine the implications of the actions you jointly need to take
- sympathise with the cause of the subordinate's inadequacy, and offer *practical* help.

Job satisfaction in employees is not easy to measure because no standard measurement criteria exist: tasks which bore some people can interest others and people might work hard even though greatly dissatisfied with their work (in pursuit of high wages for example). Some firms issue questionnaires to employees asking them to list in rank order the tasks they find particularly tedious and/or unpleasant. Equally, employees might be invited to comment on the working conditions they regard as most attractive (security, good interpersonal relations, responsibility, control over work, etc). Results from such surveys may help in designing jobs, though many of the workers' suggestions will in practice be unattainable and again the problem arises that individuals will be subjective in their response, so that jobs designed according to the suggestions of one set of incumbents might not be suitable for the next.

It seems reasonable to assume that if employees are dissatisfied in their work they will take the maximum time off. Perhaps therefore the best indicators of job satisfaction are punctuality among employees, low rates of absenteeism and labour turnover. Other important symptoms are the incidence of invocation of grievance procedures and the frequency of arguments among the staff.

Self-check

What action do you take when you identify a lack of job satisfaction in a member of your staff?

Answer
Hopefully, none of you would take no action at all. Discontent can spread very easily and affect the performance of the whole section.

Essentially, you have to identify the root cause and if a remedy can be found, implement it.

Participation

Participation in taking decisions that affect individuals' working lives can greatly motivate them to increase effort. At the organisational level, participation may occur via works' committees, advisory groups and quality circles and through other formal joint consultation procedures. Essentially, joint consultation is a communications exercise; management retains control over the decision making process, but seeks to utilise the expertise, energy and initiative of the workforce in decision making activities. Management informs employees of its plans and opinions on various issues and invites comment. The advantage to management is that expert advice is obtained from employees who possess detailed knowledge of shop floor procedures and conditions. Also, workers who exert limited control over their environments are likely to cooperate with management and be receptive to change. Note however that workers will not be happy with consultative procedures if they are invoked only when difficulties arise, especially if financial economies are needed. Joint management/worker decision taking should extend to *all* aspects of the firm's work, not just the areas it finds convenient.

Suggestion schemes might be useful for motivating staff, though problems occur in deciding who is to receive the financial benefits that result from profitable recommendations. In general, the patent rights of a new invention belong to the firm that employs the inventor, not the individual worker. Also, once a suggestion has been submitted it becomes known to the firm and it might be impossible subsequently to prove the true identity of the inventor. Indeed, a firm might initially reject a worker's suggestion only to take it up after the worker has left the organisation without rewarding that person. Nevertheless, suggestion schemes are popular with both management and workers and firms introducing them often experience large benefits.

Participation, of whatever form, has advantages and drawbacks. The principal argument in its favour relates to its mobilisation of the talents, resources, experiences and expertise of junior staff who are positively encouraged to develop their decision making capacities. People can influence the events that determine their working lives — they feel involved, useful, valued and secure. Management is forced to think hard about the implications of its actions for the staff and analytical approaches to decision taking are encouraged. Further benefits could be greater willingness by workers to abide by decisions they helped to make and the fact that bad, unworkable, decisions are less likely because those who would have to implement them receive opportunities to point out potential difficulties.

On the other hand, participation interferes with managerial prerogative, it delays decisions and can lead to inefficient working methods. Workers, moreover, rarely possess the administrative and problem solving skills needed for effective management. Other criticisms of participation include the following:

- much managerial information is confidential — often involving personal matters relating to individuals — which should not be disclosed to employees
- conflicts of interest between management and labour are inevitable, and are best resolved through collective bargaining. Workers cannot simultaneously represent their colleagues *and* be part of management
- participation does not alter fundamental financial realities. Businesses sometimes fail despite extensive prior consultation
- workers sometimes adopt short-term and mercenary approaches to complex issues which really require long-term consideration.

Self-check

What is meant by participation?
   To what extent is participation encouraged in your firm? Are there any ways in which you could encourage your staff to participate in the decision-making process of the department?

Answer
Participation is an approach to management, whereby employees are encouraged to contribute to the running of the organisation. This can range from formal joint consultative committees to suggestion schemes.
   This is a difficult problem as it can be a matter of company policy and individual managers may not have the freedom to encourage worker participation.
   Although this approach may bring benefits, all parties have to have a positive attitude. The workers must be willing and able to contribute and, moreover, believe that management will pay more than lip service to their contributions.

If participation is to succeed, both management and workers must want it to succeed. Hostility from either side guarantees failure. At the departmental level, participation involves seeking advice from subordinates, exchanging information, joint determination of targets and joint planning and control of activities. For participation to work you need to be *seen* to be willing to share your decision making powers, yet formally established procedures are not necessarily most appropriate for achieving this objective, indeed they can be counterproductive if management representatives only grudgingly and reluctantly join a formal participation system. Ad hoc joint decision making together with regular briefing sessions might be more effective in generating feelings of involvement.

Note that some of your subordinates might not want to participate in decision taking and that others may not possess the skills and experience necessary to be able to do so. Do not force people to become involved in a participation scheme and recognise that even if they are willing to offer suggestions their contributions might not have much value in the early stages of the process. Joint decision taking implies shared responsibility for jointly determined decisions, and some employees (especially those who represent others, eg union shop stewards) may not be happy about this.

Promotion

Apart from improvements in pay and conditions of work, the most immediate incentive available to an employee is the possibility of promotion. If the firm has trained its staff adequately and ensured that their work experiences are sufficiently wide, internal promotion should present no problem. External recruitment should be necessary only for specialist positions or when no-one within the organisation possesses appropriate qualifications for a post. Promotion prospects offer significant motivation.

The criteria used in selecting individuals for promotion can be based on ability or seniority. Ability related systems accelerate the careers of exceptionally competent staff, whereas seniority based procedures ensure steady progression for all employees. Knowledge that promotion is reasonably assured can improve morale throughout the entire organisation. Promotion follows logically from training, performance appraisal, management development and management by objectives programmes. People can be selected for promotion directly, management simply appointing chosen employees to higher posts, or vacancies can be advertised within the firm. Direct selection is quick, inexpensive, and suitable where management knows the abilities of all its subordinates. Internal advertisement is appropriate in large firms where several candidates of about the same level of ability might apply.

Equal opportunities considerations

Unfair discrimination in promotion upsets and demotivates staff and should always be avoided. Promotion should never be denied on grounds of race or sex. Indeed, discrimination in selection for promotion on these grounds is illegal under existing sex and race discrimination legislation. The Equal Opportunities Commission Code of Practice on avoidance of sex discrimination recommends (paras 25(c) and (d)) that promotion procedures be thoroughly examined to ensure that traditional qualifications are actually relevant to the job under consideration. It suggests, moreover, that promotion based on length of service could amount to unlawful indirect discrimination since women typically have shorter lengths of service through time out of the labour force taken for child-raising responsibilities. Where 'general ability and personal qualities' are the main requirements for promotion the Code insists that care be taken 'to consider favourably candidates of both sexes with differing career patterns and general experience'.

Organisations that operate in sensitive multicultural or multiethnic environments sometimes monitor the consequences of their promotion policies by checking whether certain groups are over represented among those who do not achieve promotion. Hence, if it is found that females, ethnic minorities or certain religious groups are prominent in the non-promoted category the reasons for this are isolated and remedial measures applied. Specifically, the following questions can be asked of the promotion system:

- what are the characteristics of non-promoted groups, and are there valid reasons explaining why individuals in these groups are not promoted?
- what contributions have non-promoted groups made to the work of the firm? Have they been adequately rewarded for their contributions?
- why do non-promoted individuals remain with the firm?
- what help can be given to non-promoted groups in order to help them qualify for promotion? What are the obstacles confronting non-promoted categories, and how can they be rewarded?
- what can management itself do to improve its knowledge of the backgrounds and difficulties experienced by non-promoted groups? How does management feel about these people?

Activity

What is your own attitude towards positive discrimination?

An analysis of those holding management positions within organisations frequently shows an under-representation of certain groups in society, ie women, disabled persons and ethnic minorities.

Positive discrimination, whereby preference is given to these groups, is seen by some as a means of rectifying the imbalance. Such a policy is fraught with problems as you may not appoint the most capable candidate and this can lead to resentment among staff.

A non-discriminatory promotion policy has numerous benefits: internal personal relationships between managers and subordinates improve, labour turnover falls (since able staff do not need to leave the firm to do higher level work) while efficiency should increase through utilisation in senior positions of the accumulated experience of long-serving employees. Additionally, there is little risk of the individuals promoted possessing unknown deficiencies, as occurs with externally recruited senior staff. On the other hand, outsiders can inject fresh ideas and apply new perspectives to existing problems, and external recruits might be of much higher calibre than internal candidates.

Activity

Have you still got the list giving reasons why people work that you compiled in an earlier activity?

Would you modify it in any way?

Now try to identify the needs that you satisfy through work and put them into a hierarchy of importance. (This may prove difficult but try it anyway.)

If you are called upon to recommend subordinates for promotion you should adhere to certain principles in making your selection. Do not overlook a suitable candidate simply because that person is performing excellently in his or her present job. It is unfair to block an individual's prospects simply because, through their hard work and personal competence, they have become indispensible in their current positions. In general, avoid promoting people who have only recently joined the firm. And always stand ready to justify your recommendations to subordinates, including those you feel are not yet ready for promotion.

Summary

You have been introduced to some of the theories of motivation and will appreciate that there can be no absolute answer to the question why do people work.

You will have your own views on how to get the best out of people but do not reject the ideas of others without first giving them some consideration.

Observe the people around you at work, particularly your subordinates, and try to keep a note of how they respond to different motivation techniques.

Several academics have made important contributions to motivation theory. Their work is described below.

Appendix — theories of motivation

Academics have for many years investigated the question of why some people work harder than others and how management can induce employees to work harder, faster and more efficiently. Motivation may be formally defined as the causal drives, needs and aspirations which determine behaviour; it can arise within the person or from outside influences, including inducements offered by the firm. Theories of motivation centre on how individuals seek to satisfy their needs, the most basic of which are physiological: food, drink, sleep and shelter. Thereafter most people experience needs for affection and contact with others; they like to feel wanted by and useful to the community in which they live and work. Higher level needs include demands for social status and personal development.

Employment satisfies many needs — wages pay for food, clothing etc and jobs bring people into contact with fellow employees. Working environments and company personnel policies can help individuals fulfil their needs, or may be sources of worker dissatisfaction. For instance, a fundamental need is for security; people seek assurances that basic requirements will always be met no matter what the circumstances. A job supplies security through tenure arrangements, sick pay and pension schemes, redundancy payments and so on. Similarly, needs for status, self-esteem and personal enhancement might be satisfied through promotion systems, participation in decision making, training and the provision of fringe benefits. Some employees are satisfied merely to exercise a particular skill, others actively seek increasing authority and responsibility, thriving on competitive authority which might take them to senior levels in their organisations.

According to F W Taylor, the founder of the 'scientific' school of management thought, workers are motivated primarily by the prospect of high wages. Thus, management should organise work as efficiently as possible in order to enable workers to earn high wages. This meant stringent application of the division of labour, work measurement and method study. Taylor did not recognise the existence of conflicts of interest between workers and their employers, believing that provided employees were offered high material rewards they would support whatever working conditions were imposed. Reactions against Taylor's approach generated a number of alternative approaches to motivation theory. The major contributions are briefly outlined below.

The work of A H Maslow[2]

Maslow suggested that individuals are motivated by five levels of need. When the first level has been satisfied the individual will attempt to satisfy second level needs, then move on to the third, fourth and finally fifth levels. The five categories of need, in the order in which (according to Maslow) a person will seek to satisfy them, are as follows.

Physiological

These must be satisfied for a person to survive. They include food, shelter, clothing, heat and light. Income from employment allows people to satisfy such basic needs.

Security

Once physiological needs have been met the individual will, Maslow argues, seek security of tenure at home and work, and protection against reduced living standards. Examples of attempts to achieve security are purchases of life, house and medical insurance and collective action through trade unions.

Social

Most people desire affection; they want to 'belong' to a community and to *feel* wanted. Hence, social groups, religious, cultural, sporting and recreational organisations naturally emerge. At work, people create activity groups, trade unions and formal and informal communication systems.

Esteem

Esteem needs include needs for recognition, authority and influence over others. Also relevant are the desire to acquire possessions and internal needs for self-respect which can be met through occupancy of highly ranked jobs and the provision of status symbols (large expensive company cars, wall-to-wall carpeting etc).

Self-actualisation

The highest level of need in the Maslow hierarchy involves creative activity and the search for personal fulfilment. Having satisfied all other needs the individual will want to accomplish everything he or she is capable of achieving, to develop individual skills, talents and aptitudes. Few people ever reach this final stage.

Maslow offers a convenient taxonomy of human needs, and he is much quoted in management studies literature. There are, however, a number of problems associated with the approach:

- some needs might not exist in certain people. What is considered important by one person could be regarded as trivial by someone else. Social environments influence individual perceptions; much depends on the traditions, cultures and life styles of the societies in which people live

Self-check

Draw a simple diagram, illustrating Maslow's hierarchy of Needs, giving an example of each level.

Answer

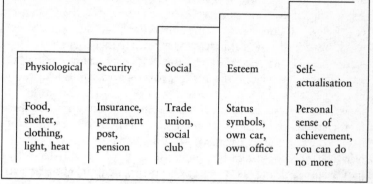

Physiological	Security	Social	Esteem	Self-actualisation
Food, shelter, clothing, light, heat	Insurance, permanent post, pension	Trade union, social club	Status symbols, own car, own office	Personal sense of achievement, you can do no more

- assuming that all the needs suggested by Maslow are in fact present, they might not be ranked in the order outlined. Needs can exist simultaneously and horizontally as well as vertically and sequentially
- Maslow had little to say about sources of needs. In fact, many basic 'needs' are learned responses with cultural rather than physiological origins. Behaviour can be conditioned; wants may be created. Equally, current perceived needs can be suppressed by social pressures
- the theory states that individuals will seek to attain higher level needs only when lower needs have been satisfied. Many people, however, are acutely conscious of 'higher' needs even though their fundamental physiological needs have not been fully met. In a consumer society, the poor may yearn for status symbols even though they are unable to satisfy their immediate requirements.

The work of F Herzberg[3]

The importance of financial reward relative to other motivating factors was investigated by F Herzberg. According to Herzberg, two separate sets of factors influence human behaviour — on the one hand people want to avoid pain and obtain the basic necessities of life, while on the other they need to develop their personal capacities and potentials. Herzberg asked professionally qualified employees (engineers and accountants) what events at work had increased or reduced their satisfaction. It seemed that the things which provided satisfaction were quite different to the things which caused dissatisfaction. Factors generating dissatisfaction were: inadequate pay, bad personal relations with colleagues, poor supervision, unpleasant physical working conditions and the absence of fringe benefits. These were called 'hygiene' or 'maintenance' factors (from the analogy that hygiene does not improve health, but does prevent illness) — they do not increase a worker's job satisfaction, but their deficiency creates dissatisfaction. Note that hygiene factors relate to the conditions of work rather than to the work itself; thus, an improvement in a hygiene factor will not be noticed for very long. For example, a worker who feels cold may complain and as a result the firm's heating is turned up, but the worker quickly becomes acclimatised to the higher temperature and forgets how cold it was in the first instance. Improvements present dissatisfaction, but do not increase satisfaction in the long run. The factors responsible for creating satisfaction ('motivating' factors in Herzberg's language) were:

- sense of achievement from completing work
- recognition from others within the organisation
- responsibility assumed
- varied work, involving an assortment of interesting tasks
- prospects for promotion.

Motivators encouraged better quality work, hygiene factors did not: a worker might resign because a hygiene element was inadequate, yet would not work harder simply because the factor was satisfactory. Likewise, the absence of suitable motivators would not cause employees to resign, but an increase in the strengths of motivating factors would significantly improve effort and performance.

Herzberg was concerned with the attitudes towards work of qualified professional and managerial staff and not with shop floor workers who might be much more concerned with prospects for immediate financial reward. Managers themselves respond to different factors in different ways. Perhaps the most controversial of all Herzberg's conclusions was that pay and fringe benefits were hygiene and not maintenance factors.

Activity

Compare Herzberg's hygiene and motivating factors. To what extent do you agree with his contention that money does not act as a motivator?

It is true that money, in particular pay differentials, is at the heart of many industrial disputes. The level of pay is seen by many as a measure of the importance, status attached to the job. Teachers, nurses in comparing their pay with that of some manual workers, feel undervalued.

There is evidence from experts such as Goldthorpe, which would seem to contradict Herzberg. Perhaps one should bear in mind that while Herzberg interviewed professional/managerial staff, Goldthorpe questioned production line workers.

Bearing in mind Herzberg's research methodology (question-naires and interviews with managerial staff) it is reasonable to suspect that many employees stated that money was not an important motivator whereas it actually was. Nevertheless, it would be wrong to overestimate the influence of the financial element. The value of Herzberg's work lies in his pointing out the importance of job satisfaction in employee motivation, though it must be said that relegation of pay to the role of hygiene factor is probably an oversimplification. Indeed, strong contrary evidence was discovered by a team of sociologists headed by John Goldthorpe[4] who conducted an extensive survey of industrial attitudes and behaviour among *manual* workers employed in three large manufacturing firms in Luton during the (prosperous) early 1960s. Two hundred and twenty-nine male operatives (and their wives) were interviewed in depth, with the investigators concluding that:

- these workers adopted 'instrumental' approaches to their jobs, seeing work as little more than a means of achieving a higher standard of living
- the workers did not expect to obtain job satisfaction; they were motivated primarily by the prospect of higher wages.

Interestingly, moreover, the interviewees still regarded themselves as 'working class' despite their enjoying relatively affluent lifestyles. Their lives at work lacked variety, autonomy and challenge, and the work itself was often undertaken in quite unpleasant physical conditions. Yet the men earned good wages which enabled them to offer their families standards and styles of living never previously experienced by manual workers. It followed that money was a great motivator to these employees.

The work of V H Vroom[5]

Vroom's expectancy theory states that an individual's behaviour is affected by:

- what the person wants to happen
- that person's estimate of the probabilities of various events occurring, including the desired outcome
- the strength of the person's belief that a certain outcome will satisfy his or her needs.

Predictions of what will happen in the future are usually based on what has happened in the past. Thus, situations not previously experienced (for example, new working practices, job changes, environmental alterations) give rise to uncertainty and may in consequence reduce employees' motivation. This is because the individuals concerned have no precedents upon which to base their assessments of the probable consequences of new situations. Hence, management should make clear to employees what precisely it expects from any alterations in policy or working practices that management might impose. Employees should be able to see a connection between effort and reward and the rewards offered should satisfy workers's needs. Vroom would argue that a complicated, unintelligible bonus scheme is unlikely to increase effort because participants cannot distinguish clear relationships between harder work and higher wages, even if higher wages are offered as part of the scheme. Similarly, experience of particular jobs gives workers precise knowledge of how output is connected to their activities. In this case expectancies are easily formed; workers know that the quantity and quality of production depends on how they perform their work. This implies that innate satisfaction derived from working hard and actually seeing the results — planned, predicted and brought about by the worker involved is a primary motivator. Of course, motivation alone is not sufficient to guarantee successful outcomes; ability is also required. Vroom suggested that levels of competence affected the relationship between performance and motivation. If a person's ability is low, then even a large increase in motivation will not cause performance to improve by very much. Equally, a poorly motivated employee of exceptional ability will not perform significantly better. Therefore, it is just as important to train and develop employees to improve their competence as it is to motivate them through offers of reward.

The work of Porter and Lawler[6]

Porter and Lawler attempt to explain the relationship between effort and performance. There are, they suggest, two factors that determine the effort a person puts into a job, firstly, the extent to which the rewards from an activity are likely to satisfy his or her needs for security, esteem, independence and personal self-development and, secondly, the individual's expectation that effort will lead to such rewards. Accordingly, the higher the person's perception of the value of a reward and the higher the probability that the reward depends on the exertion of effort then the greater the effort the individual will devote to an activity. The efficiency of a person's effort depends, the authors argue, on his or her ability (skills, intelligence, etc) and on that person's interpretation of his or her role in the organisation.

Another influential writer in the motivation field is Douglas McGregor, whose work is dealt with elsewhere. All motivation theories, however, suffer the disadvantage that they are difficult to apply in practice. They have *implications*, but rarely offer practical prescriptions for motivating employees. Herzberg's theory, for example, suggests that job enlargment will enhance motivation; but applies only to professionally qualified managerial staff — manual workers may (or may not) be motivated by entirely different factors!

Notes

1. Mintzberg, H, *The Structuring of Organisations*, Prentice-Hall, 1979.
2. Maslow, A H, *Motivation and Personality*, Harper, New York, 1954.
3. Herzberg, F, *Work and the Nature of Man*, WPC, 1966.

4. Goldthorpe, J H, Lockwood D, Beckhhofer F and Platt J, *The Affluent Worker: Industrial Attitudes and Behaviour*, Cambridge University Press, Cambridge, 1968.
5. Vroom, V H, *Work and Motivation*, Wiley, New York, 1964.
6. Porter, L W and Lawler, E E, *Managerial Attitudes and Performance*, Irwin-Dorsey, Homewood, Illinois, 1968.

6
The Management of Efficiency

Objectives

This chapter will help you to:

- understand the need for flexibility in working practices and the problems that flexibility involves
- arrange the layout of work areas so as to ensure maximum efficiency
- operate efficient cost control and just-in-time operating systems
- apply modern approaches to quality management systems, in particular quality circles.

Work study is the critical analysis of work with the intention of increasing the productivity of equipment, systems and personnel. It has two aspects: method study, which concerns how work is performed and work measurement, which is about the evaluation of the time taken to complete an operation or series of operations. Method study seeks to simplify work, eliminate unnecessary tasks, and avoid duplication of effort. It requires the systematic investigation and recording of existing and proposed work routines, and practitioners frequently advocate a 'six-step' procedure for such purposes. Firstly, the tasks to be studied are *selected*. The objectives of the investigation are defined and the problems needing solution pinpointed (eg uneven flows of work, high manufacturing costs, excessive amounts of defective production). Secondly, current methods are *recorded* and their shortcomings analysed. Thirdly, these methods are *examined*. The work is resolved into its constituent parts; duplication of effort is (hopefully) identified so that tasks can be combined and unnecessary duties eliminated.

Fourthly, new and better ways of doing the work are *developed*. The next stage is to *install* the revised methods, which requires consultation with interested parties and the alignment of new methods with existing procedures. Lastly, the new system must be *maintained*: its performance is monitored, results are compared with past experience.

Much method study is undertaken using flow-charts which highlight major and minor sequences of activity and relations between them.

Flow-charts are especially important for 'organisation and methods', which is the application of work study to (largely) clerical and administrative procedures. O and M is a specialised field, concentrating on form design, the origin and processing of documents, information storage and retrieval and the effective use of modern office technology. The major aim usually is to speed the flow of documents between people and departments, eliminating as much unnecessary paperwork as possible. Many O and M exercises consist of a series of questions, notably the following.

What is presently being done?

Information on current methods is available through direct observation, documentation and records, and from conversations with operatives and supervisors.

What is the purpose of each activity?

Are operations connected? Sometimes, activities originated through work undertaken in departments which have long ceased to exist, but the activity continues simply because those responsible for it are ignorant of its initial purpose.

Who performs each operation?

What special skills, extra training or experiences are required for particular tasks? Must a task be performed by a specific person, or will anyone do?

Where does activity take place?

Which departments are involved? Is work freely interchangeable between sections? Do operations have to take place in particular locations and if so why?

When are operations performed?

Is initiation of one activity dependent on completion of another? What are the likely consequences of failure to perform activities on schedule?

How are operations completed?

What equipment and other resources are necessary? Are alternative methods available?

What are the costs of individual operations?

What are the costs of materials, labour, and overheads? What savings are anticipated from the introduction of new methods?

The answers to these questions should reveal avoidable delays, bottlenecks, sources of error and duplication of activities. Then, measures can be introduced to regulate the flow of work, improve interdepartmental communication, reduce the number of documents transmitted between sections and generally increase the effectiveness of management control.

Self-check

What is the difference between work study and O and M?

Answer

The objectives of both are the same: to improve the efficiency with which a task is carried out. The basic difference is in the nature of the work being studied. While O and M tends to concentrate on clerical and administrative procedures, improving the design and processing of documents and information, work study concentrates on manual tasks where there is an end product.

Efficiency in production

Modern approaches to production management emphasise the need for flexibility, both in the use of equipment and in working practices. Increasingly, the layouts of configurations of equipment allow for changes in the order and character of operations, thus enabling outputs to be varied periodically. Most new systems rely heavily on robots for the completion of routine manufacturing duties. Today's robots are reprogramable, meaning that the same robot may be used for several different purposes: assembly line work (grasping and machining for example), materials handling, clearing up the workplace, spray painting, etc.

Flexible working practices require employees who possess attitudes and perspectives that make them willing to assume personal responsibility for workplace problem solving and quality control. Workers must be committed to the enterprise, capable of exercising initiative, and amenable to change. 'Lean production' (ie, the family of manufacturing processes that seek to minimise waste while maximising the quality of output) can succeed only if:

- the firm has stable industrial relations (a handful of workers can disrupt the entire production process in, say, a just-in-time system);
- the workforce is multiskilled;
- managers are well-qualified and themselves adopt flexible approaches;
- there is regular training of workers. Note how the use of robots can actually increase employees' skills requirements, *via* multitasking, the need to undertake wider ranges of duties, greater workplace autonomy, and so on.

Activity

Take a close look at the layout of an office or work area — try to choose one where several people work. Assess the following aspects of the environment and write a brief statement on each:
— accessibility (room to move between desks etc)
— lighting
— heating
— ventilation
— colour scheme
— standard of decoration (cleanliness, state of repair etc)
— furniture (style, comfort, safety)
— location of equipment
— location of people
— noise levels.

Try to be objective. The aim of the exercise is not to find fault. When you have completed the activity, continue to read through the chapter, where the problems of poor working environment are discussed.

Ergonomics and workplace design

Ergonomics concerns the relationships of people with their working environments and how these can be adapted to meet human needs and capabilities. Practical applications include the lighting, heating and ventilation of offices and factories, acoustics, design of instruments and controls and design of office furniture. A major function is the study of factors that cause fatigue at work and hence the creation of working conditions conducive to prolonged, energetic, activity. Poor lighting, for example, is not only psychologically depressing but also causes errors of judgement. Light, in conjunction with decor and colour, can affect the mood of a workplace and consequently the temperaments of workers. Cool colours in a hot environment, or warm colours in a cold one, can significantly affect output levels. Similarly, extremes of temperatures or humidity are bad for the nerves and affect the pace of work.

It is important to arrange work in such a manner that movements are minimised and/or made less tiring. This is possible through avoidance of motions requiring use of the entire arm and shoulder and motions which involved only the fingers. Tools and work materials should be positioned in appropriate ways and machinery should be designed to minimise the physical effort necessary for its operation.

Tiredness is often caused by unbalanced movements. Simultaneous, symmetrical use of both hands produces more work in the longer term than using just one hand at a time. Also, regular repetition of movements develops great speed. The establishment of 'rhythm' means that operatives do not have to think too much about what they are doing. This elimination of hesitation accelerates the movement cycle and reduces fatigue. Note however that inefficient movements can themselves become bad habits which, subsequently, are hard to break. In general, smooth continuous movements are preferable to jumpy uneven ones because they require less muscular tension and are less tiring.

There exist general principles of workplace layout and design. Handling time might be reduced by eliminating or combining operations, by shortening journeys, redesigning packages to facilitate easy handling, providing chutes and conveyor belts, and so on. Generally, control panels, tools, supplies of raw materials and components should be arranged in semicircular forms which enable application of the principles of efficient human body movement.

Machinery and equipment can be arranged according to product or process. Product based factory layout involves grouping together in one location all the equipment needed to manufacture a particular good from start to finish. The close proximity of different stages in the production process will cut waiting time between processes, reduce materials handling costs and quickly identify production line breakdowns. Process layout places alongside each other all the firm's machines and equipment concerned with a certain type of work. The advantages here are that skills are developed within specialised areas and labour trained on one machine can quickly be put onto others should breakdowns occur.

Similar considerations apply to the design of offices. A major limiting factor here is the amount of space available. 'Open plan' offices, where several functions are undertaken simultaneously in one large office, conserve space because of the absence of separating walls. Also, layout is flexible and can be arranged to facilitate the easy flow of work. On the other hand, open plan offices are noisy and expensive to heat, there is little privacy and staff can feel unimportant and uninvolved. More practically, colds and influenza present greater problems in large open plan offices than in isolated units. To make open plan offices appear more compact, screens, partitions and filing cabinets can be strategically positioned to break up 'empty' atmospheres. Noise can be reduced by proper carpeting, the use of sound deadening wall coverings, and appropriate acoustic configurations. Attention to such detail (sometimes referred to

---

Activity

What sort of office do you work in — open plan or smaller isolated units? To what extent do you agree with the statements that have been made in the text?

Modern work environments tend to favour the open plan design, with large work areas, broken into smaller stations using filing cabinets, movable partitions etc. Open plan can bring greater flexibility and most of the problems can be minimised.

---

as 'panoramic' office planning) is expensive, but staff morale and productivity might eventually be higher. Other factors that determine the character of an office environment include lighting and heating schemes, use of colour in the decor and the adequacy of ventilation. Workflow planning is an essential

Activity

Your department occupies a large open plan office recently created from several smaller ones. Furniture and fittings are brand new and there are large windows with double glazing. Staff operating VDUs begin to complain of headaches, back-aches and constant tiredness. The office is hot, very noisy and there are many distractions. Windows can only be opened from the bottom, and, when this is done, papers blow away. The canteens, restrooms and toilets are in an adjacent building. Productivity within your department begins to fall.

What actions will you take?

Answer

To improve the situation, you need to identify the links between the office environment and decreased performance. Problems include the noise, heat, lack of rest and drinking facilities and screen glare from VDUs.

Solutions could involve the installation of anti-glare shields, monitoring of how long any one person might be sitting at a VDU, strategic positioning of fans and the installation of a drinks machine. Sound-absorbing acoustic screens and carpets might also be introduced.

element of office design. Time spent on the movement of people and documents should be minimised. Thus, staff who process a particular document should if possible be close together and the equipment needed for the document's processing should be positioned nearby. It is essential that one person's in-tray not be empty while the out-tray of the employee immediately preceding in the work processing chain is full.

The systematic analysis of work has many advantages: higher output, less wasted materials, smooth production flows, lower labour costs, less time spent on handling materials and better use of existing plant and machinery. But there are many difficulties associated with implementing the results of efficiency improvement exercises. Employees will naturally fear for their jobs, or at least suspect they will have to work harder for the same wage.

Discuss all aspects of the intended new system and ensure that union or other staff representatives are involved. Explain carefully the evaluation criteria that will be used for measuring workers' performances. Disputes and grievances are common during efficiency improvement exercises, so remind your staff at the outset of the grievance and appeals procedures that currently exist. Note also that a recognised trade union is legally entitled (Employment Protection Act 1975, s 17(1)) to demand the disclosure of records, documents and information relating to a work study exercise that are relevant to collective bargaining over pay and conditions.

Cost control

You should constantly seek to cut the costs of operating your section or department, but only within reason — excessive short run cost cutting can lead to much inefficiency in the longer term. (If in doubt about whether to reduce a particular service or activity, simply ask yourself what you would do if your own personal money was used in providing that service to the firm.) First you need to establish how departmental costs are incurred and to do this effectively you need to define appropriate cost centres to which expenditures may be ascribed. These could be the activities undertaken by sections (packaging for instance), processes or assembly lines, particular products, machines or vehicles, offices, or individuals. Select your cost centres according to the ease with which you will be able to measure expenditures and exercise control.

Next, devise a comprehensive scheme for categorising costs. Distinguish between direct expenditures immediately absorbed by a cost centre (eg raw materials and machinists' wages attributable to a product) and indirect costs such as lighting, heating, secretarial support and other overheads. Then establish rules for apportioning overheads, say in proportion to the direct expenditures incurred by cost centres. Your overhead apportionment system is necessarily subjective — you could just as easily relate overheads to sizes of section measured by numbers of employees, or to volumes of sectional output — but as long as you are *consistent* you should be capable of analysing cost movements through time and comparing various costs.

Effective cost cutting depends as much on the adoption of an appropriate frame of mind as on particular measures. It is useless to cancel the departmental copy of the *Financial Times* while ignoring escalating costs of (say) entertaining customers or servicing company vehicles. Hypocrisy in these respects creates cynicism and resentments which eventually cause cost cutting initiatives to fail and it is essential that you induce your subordinates independently to participate in cutting costs. They must *want* to switch off lights, conserve energy, economise on travel expenses etc themselves. Accordingly, campaigns that originate at the base of the organisation — perhaps via quality circles, works committees, suggestion and worker participation schemes — are more likely to be effective, although senior management must always set a conspicuously good example to those it controls.

Cost reduction programmes should be particular rather than broadly defined. Target cuts should relate to specific activities or other cost centres than apply overall (eg through a vague objective to cut total costs by five per cent in the course of a year). Then, cost cutting can be incorporated into management by objectives systems and individual managers' performances may be appraised in part against the successes they achieve in cutting costs. Also, spreading the responsibility for cutting costs among many named individuals creates great cost awareness within the firm. Incentives for discovering new cost reduction possibilities might also be worthwhile (prizes, a percentage of the saving, special sectional bonuses etc).

Cost cutting needs to be carefully planned and detailed records of successes achieved (or failures) must be maintained. And programmes must be carried through. If particular cost reduction targets are not attained a detailed explanation of each shortfall should be supplied. Standardisation of parts and rationalisation of products can reduce costs greatly (although the latter has important marketing implications). Similarly, reductions in services offered (acceptance of returned items, repair and maintenance facilities, free delivery, etc) can save money, especially on slow moving relatively unprofitable items. Cuts may be sought in the following areas.

Production

Value analysis (see below) is extremely useful for cutting production costs. Otherwise, labour utilisation is (obviously) important, as are indirect labour costs: training, personnel, record keeping and so on. Perhaps jobs can be deskilled to enable lower paid unskilled employees to perform them adequately. Do skilled workers spend much of their time doing unskilled work? Can work be cheaply subcontracted to outsiders? Might overtime working be reduced, or the extra work be undertaken by part time staff paid the standard rate? You need to identify sources of machine breakdown and implement measures to avoid these interruptions (eg by planned maintenance). Look for ways to reuse scrap and waste materials, say for training purposes or for use as packaging. Are the present levels of quality of inputs and output really necessary?

Self-check

Why is it important for costs to be controlled?

Answer

There are many logical reasons for controlling costs and the following is only meant as a guideline.

A major contributory factor to the price of a product is how much it cost to manufacture or purchase. Failure to monitor costs and ensure they are kept to a minimum will result in unnecessary increases in price (which may make your product less competitive) or cuts in profit margins. The degree to which you are involved in cost control will depend largely on the policy of your organisation. The modern trend is to involve as many levels of staff as possible, since awareness of the need to control costs is the first step in achieving that goal.

Purchasing policies should be examined critically. Would bulk purchasing at a discount outweigh the costs of storage and materials deterioration? Is there a proper search procedure for ascertaining lowest cost sources of supply?

Marketing

Special problems apply here because certain aspects of marketing, especially advertising and other means of sales promotion, themselves generate income. A reduction in advertising is likely to reduce sales. However, the effectiveness of current advertising should be regularly assessed, and distribution and transport costs cut to the bone. Specific marketing functions that should be carefully examined for possible cost reductions include:

- packaging materials and equipment
- warehousing costs
- costs of discounts and special offers
- salespeople's expenses.

Sales staff paid on a time basis can be extremely expensive, since a salesperson who does not sell contributes nothing to the firm. The efficiency of the sales force should be monitored continuously, analysing the number of calls they make, costs per call, costs per order, the order/call ratio and the average profit contributed by each salesperson per month. Sales staff sometimes forget how expensive it can be to obtain an order — commission systems based on unit profitability per order rather than sales revenue or sales volume achieved might help overcome this problem. Other marketing cost savings might be possible through increasing salespeople's territories (and rewarding them for their extra work), through better route planning and through analysing the returns on visits to various categories of customer in order to reduce the call frequency in appropriate cases.

Note (importantly) that small orders are relatively expensive to process. Costs of invoicing, credit control, packaging and despatch can make small orders financially not worthwhile. Equally, the costs of providing after-sales service to small consumer units can be alarming. Discounts, transport costs and the risk of bad debts may result in certain customers not being worth the effort involved in supplying their orders.

Administration

Photocopying costs can be frightening and excessive use of a photocopier must be actively discouraged. One unnecessary cost arises from taking too many copies — 20 when only 17 are needed, a round 100 instead of 83. Multiply these extras by the cost per copy and the frequency at which the practice occurs and you have a substantial opportunity for cutting costs. To avoid this needless expense you might display a prominent notice on the photocopying machine reminding staff only to take the copies they need, or have all copying done by one person who is aware of the problem or have a restriction on the number of copies (say 10) that anyone can take without permission. Any spare copies that are accidentally taken should be used for note paper.

Self-check

The cost of one photocopy or a quick local telephone call is small, a matter of a few pence. Why is it necessary to control these trivial costs?

Answer
Small amounts soon add up and unnecessary photocopying or using equipment for personal reasons will involve organisations in avoidable costs, perhaps running into thousands of pounds.

However, the method of control itself should not involve excessive expense and human effort, or it will be self-defeating.

Activity

How does your organisation prevent unnecessary photocopying, personal telephone calls etc?

Essentially, one has to try to educate the workforce. Notices and memos stating that only a maximum of 20 copies of an item are allowed are frequently ignored. The biggest deterrent may be the fear of being found out, so if you can identify the volume of photocopying done by one person (perhaps by a personal code number to operate the machine) or the telephone calls made (by keeping a record) this may make people think more carefully.

Ideally, the workforce should be willing participants in any effort to control costs and in the long term education is the best policy.

Letters are expensive. Typing is the major cost involved, so wherever possible encourage staff to write notes on compliment slips to accompany enclosed documents rather than having separate letters typed.

Cutting administrative costs is important, but recognise the constraints involved. In most private companies administration accounts for less than 10 per cent of total costs, so saving a few photocopies or making the sécretaries use their typewriter ribbons for a little longer will not contribute much to total profitability in the long run. It is perhaps better to identify the really big sources of expenditure (raw materials, labour, processing, distribution) and seek economies there.

Fraud, theft and cheating

Supervisory managers should be aware of the possibilities for petty theft that exist in every organisation. Goods may be sent to non-existent customers, stores might be pilfered, cheques could be issued to non-existent employees and there are a thousand and one other ways of stealing from a firm. A common type of theft — weighbridge fraud — occurs as lorries leave the business. More goods are loaded than are recorded and are then driven through the factory gate. To avoid this, all vehicles should be weighed on entry to and exit from factory premises. Two difficulties arise: possible collusion between fraudulent drivers and members of the weighbridge staff and unscrupulous drivers adding unnecessary weights to vehicles on entry to the business. These extra weights (for instance, barrels full of water, spare wheels, lumps of rock, rubble, etc) are discarded within the factory and replaced by stolen goods — especially loose raw materials — of equivalent weight. Accordingly, weighbridge staff should be changed frequently and lorries should be loaded and unloaded in clearly visible areas. All heavy items on vehicles at the moment of entry should be noted to ensure they are still there when vehicles leave. The same number of passengers should be in a lorry when it leaves as were there when it entered.

Where financial transactions are involved it is probably better to have different people performing different functions (sales records and cheque issue for example) and to change the personnel undertaking these tasks regularly and without notice.

For further information on theft, see Volume 1, Chapter 10.

Value analysis

The purpose of value analysis is to reduce production costs by ensuring that every feature of a finished product serves a useful and necessary purpose. It involves the systematic study of the *functions* of the item being produced. A product's functions are the characteristics that make it operate properly (eg lift a weight, transport an item, heat a room or whatever). Functions are examined in detail, using predetermined procedures and are then related to production costs. Production engineers ask the question 'what is this item intended to do?', and then ask 'is there a cheaper way of achieving this aim?'. In consequence, the product might be redesigned or cheaper components might be used in its manufacture, or its method of manufacture may be altered. Cost reductions might be possible through buying certain input components rather than making them within the

firm. Certain quality standards might not be crucially important in terms of fulfilling a specified function.

Products that consist of many component parts are more
likely to benefit from value analysis than are single unit items,
since multi-component products offer greater scope for cost
reduction through removal of unnecessary functions. Throughout the analysis, design engineers will be seeking to reduce the
number of parts used in manufacture and to discover cheaper
alternative methods and components. Note however that for
certain products (luxury motor cars for example) high quality
fittings and components contribute to the image and conse-
quent appeal of the product even though they may not be
strictly necessary. Thus, the 'esteem values' of inputs must also
be considered when conducting a value analysis.

Self-check

What is meant by value analysis and esteem value and how do
they affect cost control?

Answer
Value analysis is an attempt to ensure that every component
part of a product is essential and that each part is 'produced' in
the most efficient, cost effective way. Esteem value may justify
the use of higher quality components than needed for the
product to function, because the buyers demand this standard of
luxury.

Just-in-time systems

With a just-in-time (JIT) system, work is planned so that each
production unit delivers to the next unit precisely the input it
requires in order to proceed with the next stage of manufacture
(or processing) and delivers the input just in time for the work
to begin. No stocks of inputs are carried, there is no bunching
of production lines or queues anywhere in the system. Successful operation of a JIT scheme requires precise scheduling of raw
materials procurement, production, processing and despatch.
There has to be a uniform daily demand throughout the entire
sequence of manufacture with minimal change-over time and
reliable equipment. Production workers themselves are

expected to operate the system — there is little defective production and inventory levels are sometimes as much as four times lower than before. This is made possible by requiring each worker to assume personal responsibility for quality and production control. Workers are organised into 'cells' which organise their own work and are put in charge of the repair and maintenance of the equipment they use, quality control, and the timing of movements of work from one cell to another.

The aim is to eliminate all spare capacity: there is no question of equipment or employees standing idle. Workers are obliged to move around completing whatever duties are necessary and helping to repair and maintain machines. Further implications of JIT are that:

- tasks are simplified in order to facilitate production (although a wide range of tasks is undertaken);
- operatives need to be proactive in identifying and dealing with problems;
- such systems are extremely vulnerable to strikes, go-slows or other industrial action by small groups of workers.

Quality management

Mention 'quality' to most British supervisors and they normally think first of statistical quality control — of tolerance and other specifications, acceptability ratios, random sampling, probability calculations and so on. British industry has tended to adopt 'scientific' approaches to quality management, involving close supervision of employees, specialisation and the division of labour, narrow job and output specifications and the frequent checking of work. Even so, the quality of output in those UK companies which apply such measures is often no better (by international standards sometimes worse) than in others. Japanese firms in particular have entirely different attitudes towards quality. There, inspection and quality control are viewed not as independent functions, but as integral and inseparable components of the *total* production system, intimately intertwined with all other aspects of the work of the firm. Production operatives assume full responsibility for quality control and no clear distinction exists between production and inspection personnel. Indeed, some large Japanese firms have dispensed entirely with specialist quality control staff and have all but abolished goods inwards inspection. Instead, they assume that suppliers will furnish high quality inputs not through fear of inspection, but as a matter of course and they issue to suppliers deliberately vague component specifications, arguing that the very act of laying down precise acceptance criteria itself implies that some defective input is acceptable provided the predetermined minimum standards are met. Excellence is taken for granted, so that inspections are seen not as a means for improving quality but as an insult to the workers concerned.

Total quality management (TQM)

The modern approach is to attempt to integrate practical techniques for controlling quality (inspection, statistical quality control, etc) with the overall strategies and tactics of the firm. In particular, TQM aims to create within the organisation a *culture* that is conducive to the continuous improvement of quality. It focuses on the totality of the system rather than its individual parts, seeking to identify the *causes* of failure rather than the simple fact that failures have occurred. Great emphasis is placed on teamwork, leadership, motivation of employees, the bonding of workers to the employing firm, and the direct involvement of operatives in solving technical and/or equipment problems.

Successful implementation of TQM requires managements to trust their workers' abilities to deal with quality problems; to train employees to undertake a multiplicity of tasks, and to provide workers with terms and conditions of employment (including long term security of employment) designed to encourage their commitment to the firm. Some companies have found it useful to identify within their workforces a number of 'quality champions' whose services can be used to facilitate the introduction of TQM methods. Quality champions are individuals who are known, liked and respected by fellow employees, and as such will be highly influential in persuading workers that TQM is a good thing. These people are far more likely to be believed than are official management communications on quality matters. Once identified, quality champions are given the information and resources necessary to help effect change. They might be invited to participate in planning the implementation of systems and in solving problems as they arise.

Workers who manage the quality of their own output save the cost of inspectors and become inescapably involved with the quality effort of the organisation as a whole. Inevitably, some defective work will occur, yet its quantity need not exceed that normally experienced when independent inspectors are employed. Note, moreover, how quality levels invariably settle just above the minimum acceptable standards whenever minimal criteria are specified.

Undeniably, inputs and outputs need inspection to protect the reputation of the firm and to improve efficiency via prevention of unnecessary work on defective materials (defectives cost just as much to produce as good items). Also, faults in machines and systems are revealed through inspection of the output they generate. The question is how inspection should occur and who should be responsible? Moreover, it is necessary to examine the *causes* of low quality. Many UK companies operate highly formal and rigorous inspection procedures, with carefully specified criteria for the rejection of work (dimensions, contents, colour, machining tolerances, numbers of allowable defectives per batch, acceptable deviations from predetermined standards etc) and employ specialist inspectors, whose work is organised on either centralised or decentralised lines. With central inspection, all items go to a central department for testing before admission to stores, despatch to customers, or passage to another stage of production. Specialised testing equipment is assembled in a single area, so that inspectors waste no time moving around departments. There is easy supervision of testing procedures and work can be dealt with on strict first in, first out principles. Flows of work within individual departments are not interrupted while outputs await inspection. However, goods must be transported to the central inspection area; handling costs increase, and goods might be damaged while in transit.

Decentralised (floor) inspection involves inspectors moving around testing materials as they are received or produced. Goods are not sent to a central area. Problems are identified where and when they occur. Floor inspection is common where heavy or bulky items are inspected or where the output from one process is needed quickly for input to another. Central inspection is appropriate if the equipment used in testing is itself heavy or otherwise immobile. Sometimes, really accurate measurement is only possible using sophisticated testing apparatus that cannot be moved from the test area.

Yet no amount of testing is guaranteed to remove the causes of defective output, which are manifold: carelessness, inexperience, poor instructions, inadequate and/or ageing equipment, bad lighting, heating or other environmental conditions, and so on. Independent testing may *identify* such problems, but they might not be cured — indeed, frictions between inspectors, departmental supervisors and operatives might actually result in reduced quality.

Quality assurance

Quality assurance (QA) is more than quality control. It concerns the total system (including the management system) needed to assure customers that their requirements will be met. QA programmes cover every aspect of the work of the firm, including the motivations (as well as the abilities) of employees, their training, experience, motivation, suitability for various tasks and so on. Formal QA standards have been drafted by various bodies, which specify that supplying firms implement definite procedures for ensuring that appropriate 'quality environments' are maintained. There are, for example, QA standards requiring that tools used on certain jobs be of a particular type and that only qualified and certificated staff be employed on certain projects.

A QA system might invite supplying firms to *improve* as well as provide contracted items and themselves to initiate alterations in the appearance, design or durability of requisitioned products. The quality of a good involves its fitness for the purpose for which it is intended as well as its physical condition on despatch. Suppliers need therefore to know the *purposes* of the articles they are invited to produce and the operational circumstances of their use, hence, a clear statement of the purpose of the item, leaving technical details (including perhaps the choice of input materials) to the discretion of the supplying firm, might have greater long term value than precise and detailed specifications of weights, sizes, machine tolerances etc. Often, QA is implemented through checklists issued to various departments asking them to scrutinise their procedures and confirm that certain measures have been undertaken. Typically, a checklist question will ask, 'What have you done to ensure that. . .' and then ask the respondent to detail the measures taken.

BS 5750

This is the British Standards Institute's quality assurance standard, which is essentially similar to the pan-European standard (EN 29000), which itself is based on a wider international standard, ISO 9000. The aim of BS 5750 is to provide suppliers with a means for obtaining BSI certificated approval that their quality management systems are up to scratch. Customers may then have confidence in a company's ability (i) to deliver goods of a prespecified quality and (ii) to maintain the quality of its output at a consistent level.

BS 5750 is a detailed and extensive document with several parts and appendices. It requires the supplier to *demonstrate* its ability to design and supply products in predetermined ways. Apart from design procedures, the specification covers the supplier's own procurement systems: its inspection and testing methods, the means by which customers may verify its claimed quality systems, how customers can check the supplier's records and other documents relating to quality procedures, and how customers may confirm the nature and extent of quality related training given to the supplier's staff. Examples of particular requirements are as follows.

- The firm must produce a quality assurance manual, with written procedures detailing:
  - internal allocations of responsibility for various aspects of quality;
  - quality control procedures, methods and work instructions; and
  - testing, inspection and audit programmes.
- Staff responsibilities for verifying quality management procedures must be (demonstrably) independent of other functions.
- Effective control over the quality of output of sub-contractors must be guaranteed.
- Design staff must possess appropriate qualifications.
- Certain quality control records must be maintained, and made available to customers.
- The firm must ensure that proper testing equipment is used.
- All the resources needed to guarantee maintenance of good quality must be identified.
- The firm must ensure that its handling, storing and

packaging procedures prevent damage to or the deterioration of goods.

- Open access to customers' representatives must be provided, and customers must be given all the inspection and other facilities necessary to verify the supplier's quality procedures.

Appendices to some of the parts of the BS 5750 contain sample questions that could be asked in order to ascertain whether a system is up to BS 5750. Examples are listed below.

- How frequently does the company conduct quality audits and how extensive are these?
- Has the firm clearly identified the staff responsible for quality control?
- Are customers' representatives given free and adequate access to inspect the supplier's quality systems?
- How are goods received inspected?
- Is the firm's test equipment up-to-date?
- How quickly are faults in the company's quality management system corrected?
- Are the firm's quality control records and work instruction documents adequate?
- Do the company's design procedures consider relevant aspects of reliability, safety, ease of maintenance, etc?
- Are crates, boxes and containers suitable for the goods?

BS 5750 (and quality assurance generally) has been criticised on the following grounds.

(a)   Firms seeking BS 5750 accreditation, *themselves* determine the level of quality of output. BS 5750 applies to the procedures for maintaining a certain quality level, even if the quality of the final output is intentionally low. Thus, a company may decide to produce rubbish, but have first class QA procedures for ensuring that rubbish is consistently generated — hence qualifying for BS 5750 accreditation.

(b)   The financial cost to a business of altering its (perhaps perfectly reasonable) quality control methods to meet BS 5750 may be colossal in relation to the overall improvement in quality that results.

(c)   Independent 'consultants' may attest that in their opinion, certain firms within which they have installed QA systems now satisfy BS 5750 standards, and issue documents to that effect. Unsuspecting members of the public might confuse such attestation with that formally recognised by BSI.

New approaches to quality management

The problem is that the very fact that management feels it necessary to query departmental quality policies implies a lack of self-confidence in the company's quality control procedures.

Self-check

How does quality assurance differ from quality control?

Answer
Quality assurance is concerned with creating an environment and management system dedicated to identifying customer needs and ensuring that the best quality product and service is given. Therefore, it will take into account documents used, attitude of staff, equipment used, as well as the end product.

Quality control relates to checking the workmanship of the final product and is an important element of a quality assurance system.

Not surprisingly, innovative firms have thus sought completely new approaches to quality management, and to look abroad for examples of how quality might be improved. A notable manifestation of this search for new methods is the attempt to apply the Japanese idea of Quality Circles to the work of British firms.

Activity

What do you understand by the term 'Quality Circle'?

We have all heard of the term and know that it is a Japanese idea, regarded by many as the secret of the success of Japanese industry in the 1970s and 1980s.

As you read on, compare your own concept of the term with that given in the text.

Quality Circles

Japanese industry has not always enjoyed its current reputation for high quality. This was especially true in the 1950s when Japanese products were frequently regarded as cheap and unreliable imitations of existing western goods. Thus, great effort was expended on improving quality in Japanese firms, and the technique of the Quality Circle was one important result. The first recorded Circle was formed in 1963 in the Nippon Telegraph and Telephone Corporation, though the idea quickly spread and soon there were many tens of thousands of Quality Circles operating throughout Japan. Today, all major Japanese companies use Quality Circles.

A Quality Circle is a departmental workers' discussion group that meets regularly to consider, analyse, investigate and resolve production and quality problems. The group is trained in problem solving techniques and, importantly, is given resources and (limited) authority to implement decisions. Circle leadership might be assumed by an existing departmental supervisor, or by someone directly elected from the group. In their western form, Circles meet during working hours (though in Japan they initially met outside the firm's time) and participation may or may not be compulsory. If membership is 'voluntary', management might encourage participation via group bonuses, generous payments for expenses, hints of promotion for enthusiastic members, overt managerial disapproval of those who do not take part etc. Circle leaders are specially trained in the techniques of group motivation and control and are made responsible for generating interest in the Circle's work among fellow employees. Circles normally concentrate on mundane practical (rather than organisational) problems and solve them using ideas and methods developed by the workers themselves. Typically, Circle activities are initiated by the Circle, although management might occasionally refer problems to the Circle for analysis and resolution.

Many large UK companies now have Quality Circles. Often, they are successful in the short run, but fail in the longer term. Morale improves initially as workers become involved (often for the first time) in decision taking, and as participants are brought together to discuss quality and productivity issues. Workers begin to take in interest in company affairs and to apply their personal knowledge, skills and experiences to the solution of quality problems. Since Circle decisions are taken by those responsible for their implementation they are almost certain to be carried out.

Eventually, however, apathy sets in as employees begin to feel they are undertaking (unpaid) extra duties, the benefits of which will accrue entirely to the firm and not to Circle members. Improved performances might not be adequately rewarded and frustrations may arise from the Circle's inability to solve problems the sources of which are beyond its control. Antagonisms develop between Circle leaders and other managers about how particular difficulties should be overcome and over the extent of the resources and executive authority the Circle should command. Within the group, friction may occur as low status, low paid employees offer more and better solutions to problems than do appointed supervisors and other higher paid departmental managers. The Circle acquires experience of participative decision making and may wish to apply this to other areas of the organisation's work (industrial relations or welfare for example), even though management might oppose employee participation apart from Quality Circles. Members then regard the Circle's terms of reference as unduly restrictive and feel that their efforts are being thwarted by higher management or others outside the group. Attendance at Circle meetings falls and meetings themselves are held less frequently. The Circle has then effectively collapsed. True, productivity and quality have improved, but one suspects that similar results might have been achieved through some other type of initiative.

Were it simply the case that quality improvement *via* Quality Circles has been prevented through management techniques not having kept pace with modern production methods the situation could easily be remedied through altering organisational structures and techniques of management control. Unfortunately, far deeper problems are involved. Note first that Japanese companies take complete responsibility for their employees' careers. There is total job security, much training and job rotation and employee participation in decision making is accepted as the general norm (activities are centred on groups rather than individuals — tasks are assigned to teams). Pay and promotion depend on length of service, so that new recruits are virtually guaranteed steady progression within the firm. Since promotion opportunities are necessarily limited, lateral transfers of workers to other departments and jobs regularly occur. Workers thus obtain a bird's-eye view of the entire organisation and are then able to relate quality problems in one section to the operations of the firm as a whole. Employees identify with the corporate personalities of their firms — all grades of worker (including managers) dress alike, eat in the same canteen and are employed under similar conditions of service. There is a single 'company union' representing all employees. Open communication between management and workers is encouraged. Much consultation between management and labour occurs and worker participation in decision taking is common. Continuous training, job rotation and acquisition of experience plus guaranteed life long employment develops in employees a great sense of loyalty to the firm, its profitability and survival. Individuals construct their long term career plans around the assumption they will progress within the organisation.

Self-check

Many UK companies, seeing the success of Japanese industries, have introduced Quality Circles, with varying degrees of success. List four reasons why Quality Circles may not bring the benefits envisaged.

Answer
Reasons given may include:
— apathy of Circle members
— lack of incentive as improved performance not rewarded
— frustration at inability to resolve problems
— antagonism between Circle leaders and management
— personality clashes within Circle
— lack of management support

Preventing Circle failure
If your firm introduces Quality Circles you will almost certainly be expected to participate, perhaps to lead the group. Accept that as an appointed manager you might be criticised by your subordinates and that your mistakes may be ruthlessly exposed. When criticism arises, concentrate on the issue; do not respond aggressively to those who voice critical views. Allocate a definite regular period for Circle meetings. If interest flags then precede Circle meetings with a short briefing on other, more

general (and hopefully interesting) issues. Make it known that you expect *all* your subordinates to attend. Provide the Circle with all the information at your disposal — if the Circle asks for more then write, on the Circle's behalf, to the manager concerned placing a copy of your letter on the departmental notice board.

To operate successfully, Quality Circles need to be considered an intrinsic part of the company's work. Ensure, therefore, that you delegate much responsibility to Circle members — Circles rarely survive long if they depend entirely on the efforts and enthusiasm of a single member. Senior management must be *seen* to support Circle activities — invite (in writing) appropriate executives to address your Circle on important matters and complain if they fail to attend. The role of the Circle must be clearly defined and all participants made aware of why the Circle was formed and the precise problems it is intended to solve. All the Circle's recommendations must be accompanied by action plans to ensure they are implemented. Keep records of who is assigned responsibility for various aspects of plans and when each objective is achieved. Disappointment is greatest when overly ambitious targets with no chance of success are widely publicised but not attained, so do not raise members' expectations to unachievable levels.

Special problems apply to Quality Circles in service industries. Many service organisations operate over several locations and their work is intangible in form. Evaluation of the costs and benefits of a service industry Circle is thus difficult since

---

Activity

Does your organisation have Quality Circles? If so, how many of the problems outlined in the text have you encountered and how were they resolved?

Perhaps one of the major factors acting against the success of Quality Circles in the UK is our work culture. In Japan, employees tend to remain with one organisation all their working lives and take a great deal of pride in the success of the company. The whole Japanese culture is also very different from our own. Therefore, while Quality Circles may have worked well in Japan, the ideas cannot simply be transported into the UK, with little thought as to their implementation.

there is no physical output to inspect. Circles in service industries typically concentrate on *systems* and *procedures*, and hence (necessarily) encroach on management functions — possibly to the annoyance of existing management staff. You should audit Circle activities periodically. How many recommendations have been implemented? What is the state of morale within the group? Are subordinates more interested in their day-to-day activities? How has management reacted to Circle proposals? Has output quality actually improved?

Ultimately, however, the long term survival of a Quality Circle depends on cultural and environmental factors beyond your immediate control. Currently, few British workers are culturally attuned to the idea that they should be personally responsible for the quality of all the output of the firm or that they should participate in production decisions. Quality management is viewed as something best left to inspectors, statistical analysts and other independent experts. Management is predominantly non-participative, hierarchical and 'top down' in approach. Instructions originate from the apex of the organisation and are transmitted downwards through rigid chains of command. Often, the establishment of a Quality Circle is a management's first ever attempt at employee participation, so that it has no experience of the difficulties that arise from participative techniques. Too often, Circles are established as ad hoc devices for improving quality and departmental efficiency rather than as a long term attempt to alter management style.

British companies do not offer life-long employment to workers regardless of the state of trade. Indeed, the overwhelming trend in recent years has been towards part time, casual and temporary work, especially among women (over half of all UK working women work part time). Operatives are recruited to do specific jobs (often on piece work) rather than as general employees; they cannot look forward to guaranteed lifelong careers. How in these circumstances can production operatives develop the sense of organisational loyalty necessary for enthusiastic participation in a Quality Circle? Couldn't-careless attitudes are endemic in casual labour systems: workers are not properly trained, they lack background knowledge of the firm and its products and are frequently paid under incentive schemes that encourage low quality output.

So long as operatives are assumed potentially incompetent, producing output that needs regular independent inspection, then few prospects exist for improving the quality of output. Negative attitudes towards employees invariably fulfil themselves; treat people as incompetent, and they will soon behave in incompetent ways. Concern for quality must be subsumed into the cultural infrastructure of the firm, and not regarded as a special or unusual function. To illustrate, contrast the manager who carefully checks every piece of correspondence that his or her secretary types, with a manager who simply signs all typed letters and memoranda without checking for mistakes. The former manager is in fact implicitly encouraging sloppy work, for the secretary will come to assume that all errors will be picked up at the checking stage and thus will take less care when preparing letters and memoranda. Certain errors will require that documents be retyped, but other mistakes will not be considered sufficiently serious to justify extra work. Thus, some proportion of documents will consistently leave the office badly typed! In the opposite case, where the secretary assumes personal responsibility for the accuracy of typed documents, high quality presentation is expected as a matter of course. To the extent that the secretary feels inwardly concerned for the quality of work, typed correspondence will always be well presented. All letters and memoranda will be near word perfect, not just some of them.

Job security, staff development, career structures for all workers, assured promotion and steadily increasing rewards, participation, respect from superiors, teamwork, regular performance appraisal and salary reviews — such are the instruments that create working environments in which employees can reasonably be expected to take a genuine and lasting pride in the quality of their work.

Summary

One of the main tasks of management, in particular at supervisory level, is to ensure that the workforce is operating efficiently. But what do we mean by efficiency? The Oxford Dictionary defines it as 'the ratio of useful work performed to the total energy expended'.

The term implies controlling the quantity and quality of work done and also the costs associated with the task. It is concerned with value for money.

This chapter has given you some insight into why the management of efficiency is important and how it might be achieved. You, as a practising manager, need to see the extent to which you can apply the ideas outlined in the text to your own place of work.

7

Interpretation of Financial Statements

Objectives

This chapter will help you to:

- understand the basic concepts and terminology of accounting
- explain a simple set of business accounts, in particular, manufacturing, trading, profit and loss accounts and balance sheet
- interpret financial information using standard accounting ratios

All managers need to be able to interpret financial information. This requires an appreciation of the meaning and significance of the data embodied in final accounts (trading accounts, profit and loss accounts and balance sheets) and the ability to comprehend cost and budget statements. Many important management functions are inextricably linked to such information and you have to be familiar with at least the rudiments of accounting data in order to control your section efficiently and communicate effectively with other members of the management team.

As a supervisory manager you both collect and receive financial information, so it is important that you understand the *purposes* for which financial statements are compiled. Two types of report must be considered: operational reports (cost analyses, outline budgets, cash flow projections etc) used for routine control and decision making; and basic end of period reports that summarise the overall performance of your employing organisation. The latter, consisting essentially of the firm's trading account, possibly a manufacturing account, the profit and loss account and balance sheet, show the extent of the business' trading activities, the rate of return it achieves and the structure of its assets and liabilities.

Activity

Since the chapter is concerned with understanding financial statements, accounts etc you will find it useful to refer to a set of your organisation's accounts, such as you might find in an annual report and any other financial information that may be available.

The trading account

A firm's trading account shows its gross profit (or loss) during a given accounting period (month, quarter, year, or whatever). The term 'gross' profit means the difference between sales revenues and the acquisition and/or direct production costs of the goods sold, before deducting the firm's administrative and other non-production expenses (though warehousing is usually regarded as a production expense in this context). Gross profit may then be compared with turnover to establish the business' average percentage markup on sales. If the markup is high and the firm still does not make a profit after allowing for expenses then the business is administratively inefficient and various cost cutting measures must be imposed. A simple trading account might appear as shown in Example 7.1.

Example 7.1

	Sales		£100,000
less:	Cost of sales		60,000
	Gross profit		40,000

where cost of sales is given by:

	Opening stock	20,000	
plus:	Purchases	50,000	70,000
minus:	Closing stock		10,000
			60,000

Here, sales receipts are £100,000 while the cost of these sales, ie opening stock plus purchases less closing stock, is £60,000. Try working out the gross profit from the following information: purchases £19,750; opening stock £1,800; stock at close £1,950, sales £24,500. The answer is £4,900. Did you get this? If not reread the few paragraph to check your understanding.

Other items may contribute to the cost of sales and should therefore be deducted from the value of sales. In certain cases the computation of the cost of sales might require the compilation of a separate 'manufacturing account'.

Manufacturing accounts

Some businesses distribute goods which they have bought already manufactured or assembled, others purchase raw materials and/or input components which are then processed by the firm. The trading account of a business that merely distributes finished goods without altering them in any way

---

Example 7.2

	Opening stock of raw materials		£100,000
add:	Purchases of raw materials		200,000
			300,000
less:	Closing stock of raw materials		50,000
hence:	Value of raw materials consumed is		250,000
add:	Manufacturing wages		250,000
			500,000
add:	Opening work in progress	50,000	
less:	Closing work in progress	40,000	10,000
			510,000
add:	Factory overheads:		
	depreciation of plant		
	and equipment	5,000	
	power	4,000	
	rent and rates	11,000	
	lighting and heating	5,000	25,000
hence:	Cost of manufactured goods is		535,000

(a retail shop for example) is compiled in a straightforward manner with the opening stock of finished goods plus purchases being deducted from sales plus stock at close in the usual way. Also deducted are any warehousing costs (warehouse rent, storekeepers' wages etc) and any other non-administrative direct expenses (depreciation on warehouse equipment for example).

For manufacturing businesses, however, the calculation of the cost of sales is more complicated. A manufacturing account contains all the costs of producing goods: manufacturing wages, raw materials consumed, factory overheads, work-in-progress completed, cost of carriage inwards, and so on. The account might be set out as shown in Example 7.2.

This value is now transferred to the manufacturer's trading account as shown in Example 7.3.

Example 7.3

	Sales		£980,000
	Cost of manufactured goods	535,000	
add:	Opening stock of finished goods	155,000	
		690,000	
less:	Closing stock of finished goods	190,000	
	Cost of goods sold		500,000
	Gross profit		480,000

All 'direct' manufacturing costs must be included in the manufacturing account. The word 'direct' in this context means there is an immediate relationship between the cost incurred and the goods being processed. Thus, direct materials are materials that become physically embodied in the goods; direct labour is the labour that actually works on the manufactured items. Indirect factory costs which, nevertheless, contribute to the cost of manufactured output (including the costs of maintenance of machines and equipment, factory cleaning, wages of supervisors and so on) are listed under the heading for 'factory overheads'.

Self-check

What costs are included on a manufacturing account? Give two examples each of direct costs and factory overheads.

Answer

The manufacturing account includes all costs connected with the manufacture of the product.

Direct costs include raw materials, machine operatives' wages, any item brought in for a specific task (eg hire of a piece of equipment)

Factory overheads or indirect costs are all the items of expenditure associated with the running of the factory, but which cannot be allocated to a specific job. Examples include factory rent and rates, factory power, depreciation of factory equipment, salaries of supervisory staff, cleaning.

As an exercise, work out the cost of manufactured goods from the following information.

	£
opening stock of raw materials	5,000
opening stock of partly manufactured goods	8,000
closing stock of raw materials	4,000
closing stock of partly manufactured goods	9,000
purchases of raw materials	30,000
carriage on raw materials	300
manufacturing wages	22,000
factory lighting and heating	2,500
factory rates and insurance	700

The answer is £55,500. If you didn't get this then reread the last few paragraphs and redo your calculations.

Stock valuation methods

Several techniques are available for valuing stocks of raw materials and input components purchased by the firm and subsequently issued for use in the production process. The 'first-in first-out' criterion, for example, assures that materials are issued from the earliest batch received until this is fully exhausted, then from the next delivery. Stock issues are valued at the actual cost price of each lot. FIFO is simple, convenient and accurate, but can be expensive to administer and may not be appropriate where purchase prices change frequently. Under the 'last-in, first-out' method the most recently purchased stock is assumed to be issued first, then the next most recently purchased and so on until the current stock is exhausted. LIFO values stock issues at nearer their current market prices than FIFO since, for example, falling raw materials prices causes FIFO to overvalue current stock usage because the stock released is valued at past, higher prices. With the 'average cost price' method the mean average unit purchase cost is computed for each stock item. Unfortunately, arithmetic means are exaggerated by extreme values and may not truly represent typical prices of stock. Thus, weighted means are sometimes used, with weights determined by the quantities purchased at each price. 'Market price' inventory valuation charges stock issues at current market prices regardless of their costs of purchase. Other possible valuation methods are as follows.

Self-check

In valuing stock what is the difference between FIFO and LIFO? What would be the effect of each on profits?

Answer

First In First Out: assumes that the oldest stock is used first, and stock issues are charged at actual cost price.

Last In First Out: assumes that the most recently purchased stock is used first, and stock issues are charged at actual cost price.

When valuing closing stock using FIFO you will be using the more recent cost prices, since the items left in stock will be those most recently purchased.

When valuing closing stock using LIFO you will be using the older cost prices, since the items left in stock will be those purchased at an earlier date.

Closing stock affects the cost of goods sold and consequently gross profit. In simple terms, the greater the value of closing stock, the higher the level of gross profit. The number of items left in stock will not vary but the valuation method chosen could affect profits.

Highest-in first-out

The lowest priced stock is held longest. This will minimise the value of retained stock. As with LIFO and FIFO, stock is valued on release at the actual cost of purchase.

Next-in first-out

This avoids the need for continuous monitoring of supply prices. NIFO values all current stock issues at the purchase price payable on the latest order placed with a supplier even if the goods have not been received. If, for instance, components are ordered in January at a price of £5 per unit for delivery in March, *every* component issued from existing stocks between January and March is assumed to have cost £5, regardless of the prices actually paid.

In selecting a particular method management will be influenced by the method's convenience, by tax considerations (high stock values mean bigger book values for working capital), and by how accurately it predicts inventory replacement costs.

The profit and loss account

The next step is to deduct administrative and certain other expenses from gross profit. This is achieved through the preparation of a profit and loss account, the result of which is the calculation of the the the net profit of the firm. Typical administrative expenses are the salaries of administrative staff, non-factory rent and rates, insurance, telephone costs, stationery and postage and office lighting, heating and electricity. Additionally, the following expenditures should be deducted from gross profit.

- marketing expenses: advertising, wages of sales staff, distribution costs, agency fees, etc
- financial expenses: discounts allowed less discounts received, bad debts, debenture interest, interest on bank loans and overdrafts
- depreciation on machinery, land, buildings, vehicles, and similar assets. (Though note that if the firm is a manufacturing business then the depreciation on factory buildings, plant, factory machines etc appears in the manufacturing account rather than in the profit and loss account)
- dividends paid and awaiting payment
- transfers to reserves.

Then, interest received on bank and other financial deposits and income from investments are added to give a figure for net profit before tax.

All the figures used in the calculations must relate strictly to the period covered. Sales are conventionally defined as goods despatched during a period (including those sold on credit), not just money received. Stocks must always be valued at cost (not market) prices for accounting purposes. Otherwise, profits will be assumed to accrue before stocks are processed and sold. Purchases (which are measured net of any returns) are usually taken as goods *actually* received during the accounting period, even if the invoices for some of them have not been settled. Depreciation is a charge against profits because it is assumed that the amounts written off will be needed for eventual replacement of assets.

Mistakes sometimes occur, unintentionally, through late invoicing by suppliers, leading to underestimation of the expenses incurred during an accounting period (a telephone or electricity bill, for example, might be received long after it became due). Thus, any expenses not covered by invoices received should be approximated and included in the accounts for the current period. Another source of inaccuracy is double counting of goods as both finished stock awaiting sale and as invoices included in the figure for sales. This can be a difficult problem in large businesses where very many invoices are issued daily. For instance, on Friday afternoon a large number of finished items may be withdrawn from stock and despatched to customers, invoices will be dated that Friday and issued the following Monday. Yet stock figures might not be updated until the end of the week after despatch, so that an accounting cut off point on, say, Tuesday will cause the items to be counted as both stock on hand and as sales. Similar considerations apply to purchases. Goods can be received and incorporated into the stock figure before invoices are received and included in the balance sheet figure for creditors.

The balance sheet

A balance sheet should inform a firm's owners (and other interested parties) of the firm's assets and liabilities, its capital structure, and whether is is solvent. The document states how the business' assets are deployed, and the sources from which the acquisition of those assets were financed. Consider the (highly simplified) example of a balance sheet for a small firm shown in Example 7.4.

The assets column shows the uses of the firm's resources, the liabilities side states how the assets were financed. Since every asset has to be paid for in some way or other the two sides must necessarily add up to the same amount – hence the term 'balance' sheet. The balance sheet summarises the firm's financial position on the date it was compiled: it is analogous to a photograph freezing a situation at a particular moment. Assets are the possessions of the business at that moment, liabilities are the people or institutions who own the assets or to whom they are owed.

Self-check

Explain the difference between the manufacturing account, the trading account and the profit and loss account. Give two examples of items you would expect to find on each.

Answer
Manufacturing accounts are only prepared by those companies which actually engage in making products. The purpose of the account is to calculate the cost of making the finished goods which were subsequently sold. Items included are cost of raw materials used, direct labour, factory light and heat, depreciation of plant and machinery, salaries of supervisory and management staff of the factory, factory rent and rates etc.

Trading accounts are used to calculate gross profit, ie the difference between revenue from sales and the cost of producing the goods or the cost of buying them in. Information used includes sales net of returns, purchases net of returns, carriage paid on goods received, opening and closing stock.

The profit and loss account takes the gross profit figure and deducts all the other expenses incurred in running the business to give the net profit for the period. Expenses might include office salaries, depreciation on cars, office equipment, telephone, electricity, rates, bank charges, travel etc.

For most businesses there are three main sources of funds: owners (shareholders in a limited company), long term loans from banks and current liabilities such as overdrafts or trade credit. Balance sheets can be presented horizontally, with assets

Example 7.4

Assets		Liabilities	
Fixed assets		*Capital*	
Land and buildings	£65,000	Shareholders' funds	80,000
Plant and equipment	35,00		
Vehicles	15,000	Long term liabilities	
	115,000	Debentures	20,000
		Bank loan	20,000
Current assets		*Current liabilities*	
Stocks	5,000	Creditors	5,000
Debtors	3,000		
Cash	2,000		
	125,000		125,000

and liabilities listed alongside each other or (more usually) vertically. Figures for the current and two previous years will usually be quoted. Difficulties arise in choosing headings for categorisation of items. Each significant component should be shown separately, but opinions differ about which items are sufficiently important to warrant an individual entry. Detail is desirable for the purposes of analysis, but might confuse the reader. Thus, many firms present broadly categorised summary data in the main published account, accompanied by numerous explanatory notes. A typical company balance sheet categorisation is outlined in Example 7.5.

Activity

Find the balance sheet in your set of accounts. Compare the layout and information with that given in the text. Do not worry if the layout is different, many companies use the vertical format (this is outlined later in the chapter) rather than the horizonal format given in the text.

Shareholders' contributions consist of share capital (uncalled share capital is regarded as an asset[1]) and reserves (because shareholders own the profits the firm has chosen not to distribute as dividends). The share premium account shows the extent to which shares were issued at prices above their nominal values. For example, if a £1 share is issued at £1.50

Example 7.5

Assets
Called up capital not paid

Fixed assets
(a) Intangible
    Goodwill
    Ownership of licences and patents
(b) Tangible
    Land and buildings
    Plant and machinery
    Fixtures and fittings
    Vehicles
    (less depreciation on fixed assets)

Investments
Equity, fixed interest and other investments held by the firm
Current assets
    Stocks (including work in progress)
    Debtors (less provisions for bad debts)
    Cash at bank and in hand
    Prepayments

Liabilities
Capital and reserves
(a) Called up share capital
    Preference shares
    Ordinary shares
    Other shares
(b) Share premium account
(c) Revaluation reserve
(d) Other reserves
(e) Balance from profit and loss account
(f) Provisions for liabilities (eg deferred taxation, provisions for pensions for employees)
Creditors
  Amounts falling due after one year
Current liabilities
(a) Creditors: amounts falling due within one year
(b) Proposed dividends
(c) Debenture interest due
(d) Bank overdraft
Loan capital
  Debentures

then £1 is shown as share capital and £0.50 as a share premium.

Self-check

Explain the following terms, without reference to the text.

— Dividend
— Share premium account
— Debentures
— Debenture interest
— Current assets
— Current liabilities.

Answer

Dividend is the share of profits made by the company distributed to the shareholders and represents a return on their investment. It is usually expressed as a percentage or as an amount per share.

Share premium accounts are used where the company issues shares at a price above the face value, say £1.15 for a 50p share. In this example 65p per share would be recorded in the share premium account.

Debentures are also known as loan stock and represent a safe form of investment. In effect the investor is lending money to the company in exchange for a fixed and guaranteed rate of interest, but sacrifices any say in the running of the company.

Debenture interest is paid at a fixed rate and has first call on any profits made. It is treated as an expense on the profit and loss account and deducted from profits before the calculation of corporation tax (unlike dividends, which are deducted after tax).

Current assets, also called circulating assets, represent short term cash or near cash with which to run the business.

Current liabilities are those debts owed by the company which fall due within the next year.

Debentures are long term loans to the company secured against its assets. The debenture document is simply a statement acknowledging the debt. Holders of debentures must be paid the interest to which they are entitled, on time and in full, even if the company has made no profits: some or all of the firm's assets may have to be liquidated to allow this to occur. Shareholders, conversely, are not legally entitled to dividends if no profits have been earned. In this case, neither ordinary nor preference shareholders receive anything at all for this period, although preference shareholders whose shares are 'cumulative' (and most preference shares are in fact cumulative) will receive their dividend payment for this year (and subsequent no-profit years) just as soon as the company once again begins to earn profits. If a small amount of profit is made, preference shareholders get their dividends before the question of a dividend for ordinary shareholders is considered.

The above categorisation is that recommended by the EU. Note however that many companies (possibly yours included) prefer to show fixed assets plus working capital (where working capital is current assets less current liabilities) rather than showing current assets in one part of the statement and current liabilities separately elsewhere.

Balance sheet analysis

Balance sheet figures may be used to form ratios indicative (hopefully) of the performance and financial status of the business. The most basic ratio is that which expresses the rate of return achieved on capital employed. Gross capital employed is defined as fixed assets plus current assets; net capital employed is fixed assets plus current assets minus current liabilities. Measurement problems arise in defining asset values, eg should assets be valued at market prices or at cost and which items are to be included in the list of 'assets'? Some firms regard cash and other idle assets as irrelevant when assessing performance, on the grounds that idle assets are not involved in profit creation.

Should goodwill be regarded as an asset when computing profitability? The value of goodwill cannot be ascertained until the business is actually sold, so that any assessment of goodwill is necessarily subjective. Yet goodwill is undoubtedly an important asset for many businesses!

Similar considerations apply to the valuation of brands, which are valuable assets in their own right. Companies can sell their brand names to other businesses for considerable sums of money, and today brand values appear as major intangible assets in the balance sheets of many firms. The problem with assessing the monetary worth of a brand is that, ultimately, the only way to value a brand is to sell it to the highest bidder, so that until a sale occurs the brand's owner has to rely on subjective factors to fix an appropriate amount. Examples of such factors include:

- an estimate of the influence of the brand name on the price at which the item can be sold;
- the effects of the brand name on consumer loyalty;
- whether the brand contributes to the firm's overall corporate image;
- the extent of the firm's past expenditures on developing the brand (advertising costs for example).

Further problems arise when defining profit, since earnings retained within the business for future investment may be thought of either as profit (which has yet to be distributed) or as a working *asset* that will be used to generate further revenues.

The return on capital employed ratio should express net profits as a proportion of the value of the assets used in their creation. It is an overall measure of the efficiency of a firm, frequently used to compare firms and industries. Stock exchange investors are greatly influenced by companies' returns on capital employed, and firms exhibiting low values for this ratio frequently experience difficulty when seeking stock exchange funds.

Another important index available from balance sheet data is the firm's 'current ratio', ie the ratio of its current assets to current liabilities. Current assets and liabilities are those which mature or are payable within 12 months. The current ratio (also known as the working capital ratio) shows the composition of the working capital of the firm and the degree of liquidity of the business. Current assets of stock, debtors and cash are immediately or easily converted into purchasing power, whereas current liabilities (trade creditors and accrued expenses) might have to be settled at very short notice thus draining the business of short term funds. Note the potential conflicts that exist between needs for working capital and for additional fixed assets — plant and equipment, vehicles, furniture — used to expand production. The ratio is written:

$$\frac{\text{current assets}}{\text{current liabilities}}$$

It is not expressed as a percentage because its purpose is to show how many times current liabilities are covered by current assets. There is no common ideal value for the current ratio; factors relevant to fixing an appropriate value are as follows:

- the extent of the firm's short term borrowing. If this is

substantial the current ratio needs to be higher so that creditors' demands for repayment can be quickly met

- how fast raw materials prices are rising. A high rate of inflation lowers the purchasing power of working capital, so that more cash is needed
- rates of interest. High interest rates mean substantial interest repayments
- the degree of uncertainty facing the business. Risky businesses require high current ratios.

Since some current assets take longer to liquidate than others it is useful to compute a ratio that measures a firm's capacity to settle its debts at short notice. The 'acid test' (or 'liquidity') ratio serves this purpose, since it incorporates only those current assets which can be instantly converted into purchasing power. Thus, stocks of raw materials and work in progress, which take time to convert into cash, are ignored. The ratio is:

$$\frac{\text{Cash + debtors + realisable investments}}{\text{Current liabilities}}$$

Note the (highly) optimistic assumption that all debtors will settle their outstanding balances on time. This in fact is an unrealistic supposition: long delays in settling debts are common and some bad debts inevitably occur. The value of the liquidity ratio should be about one, meaning that current

---

Self-check

Explain the difference between the current ratio and the acid test.

Answer

Both are concerned with the short term viability of the company and its ability to cover current liabilities.

Current ratio is current assets: current liabilities

While many textbooks give the norm as 2 : 1, it depends largely on the nature of the business. Ideally, as with all interpretation of accounts, you should calculate the figure over a period of time, say five years, and look for a trend.

Acid test ratio is current assets less stock: current liabilities

The objective is to see whether those assets readily convertible into cash, will cover short terms calls on funds represented by current liabilities. Again the norm of 1 : 1 must only be regarded as a general guide.

liabilities are fully covered. Values exceeding one are undesirable because surplus liquid funds should always be invested in alternative and profitable uses.

The current ratio can be broken down into its constituent parts. For example:

$$\frac{\text{stock}}{\text{current assets}} \qquad \frac{\text{debtors}}{\text{current assets}} \qquad \frac{\text{cash}}{\text{current assets}}$$

and likewise for elements of current liabilities.

Balance sheet data used in conjunction with information taken from trading and profit and loss accounts can support other analyses. For instance, excessive stockholding is revealed in low values of the 'stock turnover ratio':

$$\frac{\text{cost of sales}}{\text{average stock}}$$

This shows the speed of inventory turnover. If, for example, the accounting period is one year and the ratio has a value of two, then on average a unit of stock is held for six months. Values lower than two mean that stock is held longer than six months (on average) and vice versa. High values are appropriate for firms which face irregular and unanticipated changes in market demand, where sudden alterations in consumer taste may cause big increases in sales. In general, the faster that stock turns over the better because rapid conversion of stock into

---

Activity

No one is expected to memorise the ratios and formulae used when interpreting financial accounts, unless that is, you are taking a closed book examination.

Take a sheet of paper and write down the ratios covered so far and make a note of those given later in the text. Refer to the sheet as necessary.

The ratios covered so far are:
— return of capital employed
— current ratio
— acid test
— stock turnover
— debtor ratio.

If necessary, refer back to the appropriate sections in the text and if need be, write brief explanations of terms you find confusing.

sales means the generation of funds which themselves lead to more profits. Usually, perishable goods have the highest turnover rates, while consumer durables and luxury goods take longer to sell. Another useful ratio is the 'debtor ratio':

$$\frac{\text{value of debtors}}{\text{annual sales}} \times 12$$

which shows the average period, in calendar months, required to collect debts.

Several indices of profitability other than the return on capital employed are available. Examples are the ratios of gross and net profit to sales, of expenses to sales and (for limited companies) of earnings per share and the share price/earnings per share ratio. The latter expresses the current market price of a share in a company as a proportion of the earnings of that share (dividends plus capital appreciation) over the last year and thus indicates how many years are required to recoup the initial investment, assuming last year's performance continues.

To illustrate these concepts consider the following simple example of a trading and profit and loss account and balance sheet for a hypothetical firm.

Example 7.6

Trading and Profit and Loss Account

	Sales	£102,000
less:	Cost of sales	82,000
	Gross profit	20,000
less:	Expenses	8,450
	Net profit	11,550

Balance Sheet

Assets			Liabilities	
Fixed assets after depreciation		£38,500	Share capital	£30,000
			Undistributed profit	11,550
Current assets			Current liabilities	
Stock	10,010			
Debtors	14,600		Creditors	22,340
Cash	780	25,390		
		63,890		63,890

Here the capital employed is £41,550 and the return on capital employed 27.8 per cent. The stock turnover rate is 8.2, and the debtor ratio is 1.72 months. Other useful ratios available from this data are:

creditors: sales	0.22
current ratio	1.14
liquidity ratio	0.69

Were you able to arrive at these figures easily? If not look back through the last few pages of text.

Capital structure

When reading a company balance sheet look carefully at the business' capital structure (ie the relative proportions of shares, debentures, and undistributed profits in the liabilities section). Shares have the advantage (from the company's point of view) that dividends need not be paid during loss making periods. Debenture interest, on the other hand, must be paid in full when it falls due. However, debenture holders have no vote and thus cannot challenge the existing management at the company's annual general meeting. Note that the risk of liquidation is higher with debenture financing since debenture interest *must* be paid regardless of current financial circumstances.

Against this background, companies have been tempted to finance themselves entirely by ploughing back their own profits, which are interest free. Unfortunately, ploughing back profits means that the asset value of a business will go up (as profits are reinvested in the firm) while simultaneously the market price of shares in the company will deteriorate: ordinary investors are not interested in buying shares in companies that pay low dividends, and dividends are inevitably lower in the short term through the firm holding back its profits. The very real danger here is that the declining share price of a financially sound company will attract unwelcome takeover attempts by outsiders, who may want the company not in order to run it, but simply for its capital assets.

The choice of the proportions of debt, enquity and retained profit to incorporate into a company's asset structure is one of the most important decisions its directors have to make. Debenture financing is appropriate for stable, low risk industries — shares are perhaps better for risky and unstable environments where profits fluctuate and money for interest payments might not be available in certain periods. Retained profits are in a sense a free resource in that no interest has to be paid on them, but they must be administered judiciously bearing in mind the share price implications of reduced dividend payments. Companies with shares that have high market values in relation to capital employed and which are earning good profits are most likely to retain substantial parts of their revenues.

Activity

Study the capital structure of your organisation: compare the proportions of debt (debentures and long term loans), equity and retained profit.

Over the years there has been considerable debate as to the optimal ratio. Debt can bring benefits, particularly in tax savings, since the cost is deducted from profits before corporation tax liability is calculated. However, as the interest payments are 'guaranteed', they have first call on any funds available.

Costing

Costing concerns the prediction and categorisation of costs, their allocation to individual products or activities, and the assessment of profitability. Costs are divided into two categories; direct costs and overheads. Direct costs are the costs of materials, labour, and other direct expenses. Overheads are costs that are not attributable to specific products. They relate to the creation of the environment in which production takes place. Examples are maintenance of buildings, rent of premises, lighting and heating, secretarial and administrative services, costs of cleaning and so on. Unlike most direct costs, overheads usually do not vary with respect to the volume of production, though in practice the categorisation of particular costs as 'fixed' or 'variable' can be difficult. Rent is clearly fixed, electricity used to power a machine is variable, but electricity used for lighting the premises which is switched on for longer periods during busy spells is partially fixed and partially variable. The sum of direct costs for materials, labour and other expenses is sometimes called the 'prime' cost of a product. Thus, final production cost comprises prime cost plus overheads.

There are problems associated with the allocation of overheads to individual items, since firms typically manufacture several products. Fixed costs must therefore be split up amongst the various products according to some predetermined criterion. Many firms define 'cost centres' to which all the costs of producing particular goods (or services) may be apportioned. Cost centres can be departments, sections of departments, processes or production lines. All direct costs are easily attributable to appropriate cost centres. Overheads, however, are not. Deciding how to allocate overheads is difficult and varying the criteria used can alter dramatically the estimated costs (and hence price) of an individual product. Before considering this question in depth we need to examine the concept of 'standard' costs.

Activity

How are fixed costs apportioned in your organisation? Are there cost centres, and if so, how many? There is no simple and equitable way, but the main methods will be outlined later in the text.

Standard costing

This applies the work study concept of 'standard' performance to the estimation of production costs. Predetermined expected values for materials usage, labour time, machine expenses etc are aggregated and subsequently compared with the actual cost of making a certain product. Differences between expected and realised costs are called 'variances'; they highlight deviations of actual performance from prior assessments of how long an item should take to produce, how much raw materials it should require and the value of the overheads it should (theoretically) absorb. Careful analysis of variances will reveal sources of inefficiency.

Overhead allocation

Indirect costs that cannot be directly charged to cost centres have to be apportioned on a pro rata basis according to some predetermined criterion. This process is called the 'absorption' of overheads by cost centres. Some overheads are easier to apportion proportionately than others. Rent and rates for example can be allocated to departmental cost centres in relation to the cubic footage of the space they occupy. Heating, lighting and cleaning may be similarly apportioned, or through the numbers of radiators, lightbulbs, or units of cleaning materials used in each section. The costs of running a works canteen can be allocated proportionate to the numbers of employees in each department, as can training costs and the costs of administering pension schemes and PAYE.

However, some service functions serve not only production cost centres but also other service activities, thus contributing to the latter's operating costs. The canteen, for instance, needs light and heating while the workers who administer these services themselves need to be fed! Complex allocation systems may ensue with the result that the final apportionment of overheads to products creates product prices which do not truly reflect actual production costs. Hence, many firms adopt simplistic but administratively convenient rules of thumb for allocating overheads. For example, they might classify overheads under a handful of major headings which are then absorbed by products according to a single criterion, such as a straight predetermined percentage of some other cost. Typical overhead categories are:

- production overheads; consisting of factory rent, heating, maintenance of equipment, supervisors' and factory office workers' wages, inspection costs etc
- marketing overheads, eg advertising costs, salespeople's remunerations and expenses, marketing research and sales promotion costs, public relations
- administrative overheads such as stationery, managers' salaries, office expenses, insurance, costs of company cars, maintenance of buildings and so on.

These overhead classes might be absorbed into products by adding some predetermined percentage of the direct cost which is most important to each product. Thus, if direct wages are the dominant direct cost in the production of a certain item then overheads are absorbed into that product by adding a percentage of the value of the wage cost to account for overheads. Different percentages can be used for different categories of overhead. This is illustrated in Example 7.7.

Alternatively, overheads might be allocated in proportion to the number of labour hours used in manufacturing various items, or to machine hours, or to some other variable. The advantages of using direct labour cost are that it (usually) reflects the time taken to produce the item and the number of employees associated with the item's production and hence their needs for support services. However, the method does not account for differences in wage rates among workers employed to produce different products or for the distortions created by overtime working.

If overheads are significantly related to materials costs then materials inputs might conveniently serve as the basis for overhead absorption. Unfortunately, materials input prices might fluctuate according to market forces while overheads remain constant, resulting in frequent over or under allocation of overheads. And high material input prices do not mean that much time or equipment are required to produce the product.

Example 7.7

Suppose the direct labour cost of producing an item is £1,000 and the firm decides to add 50 per cent for production overheads, 20 per cent for marketing overheads and 10 per cent for administration; then we have:

direct labour	£1,000
production overhead	£500
marketing overhead	£200
administrative overhead	£100
	£1,800

Add this to the product's direct material cost and we have the total production cost of the item. In choosing these percentages the firm must ensure that the total values of the three classes of overhead 'are fully recovered by absorption into products. If materials cost is the dominant direct cost then overheads could be expressed as percentages of this rather than the cost of direct labour. Note how a change in the percentages applied alters (somewhat arbitrarily) the estimated final production cost — and hence the selling price — of the product.

Costing systems

Job costing means estimating the cost of a specific order. Each order is different and made to a particular (probably unique) design. Examples are book production, engineering and construction projects and repair services (motor car repairs for instance). Contract costing is used by building and construction firms and others who work to specific contracts for projects. Costs are based on the location (site) of the project which may or may not be the supplying firm's own premises and certain jobs might be sub-contracted to outsiders. Penalties may be incurred if work is not completed on schedule. Batch costing applies to firms where goods are produced in batches, eg shoes or items of clothing. Costs accrue to each batch rather than to each item. Total batch cost is then divided by the quantity to give the cost per unit.

Self-check

Identify three different ways in which overheads might be allocated to cost centres.

Answer

The problem with overheads is that they cannot be clearly identified with particular cost centres. Therefore it is necessary to find some way of sharing them between the cost centres in a fair and equable manner. But this is often easier said than done.
   Possible methods include:
— equal distribution between the cost centres
— based on the number of staff in each cost centre
— based on the floor space in each cost centre
— based on the value of plant and machinery in each cost centre
— based on a pre-determined percentage of a direct cost.
   Fixed (direct) costs have to be paid by the organisation and the purpose of sharing such costs between the various departments is to ensure that they are taken into account when calculating the total cost of production.

Process costing relates to continuous flow methods of production — chemicals and steel for example. With process costing it is not possible to charge costs to specific units of output, so the average cost of the product is computed through dividing the direct costs attached to the product during a certain time period and then adding overheads according to some formula.

Marginal costing

This involves distinguishing between fixed and variable costs of production. Only variable costs (prime cost plus variable overheads) are allocated to cost units; fixed costs are attributed to the business in general and recovered from the differences between the selling prices and variable costs of products. These differences are called the 'contributions' of products and, since they depend on selling prices, fluctuate according to market forces. Thus, no profits occur until total contributions exceed total fixed overheads. The point where contribution and fixed overheads are equal is referred to as the firm's break-even point. This approach avoids the need for the arbitrary allocations of overheads inherent in the 'full cost' methods previously discussed.

Budgets

Budgets compare actual costs and achievements with planned achievements and allocations of financial and other resources and are probably the most widely used of all methods of financial control. Upper spending limits (or minimum performance standards — sales or production levels for instance) are specified for each of a number of functions (purchase of supplies, secretarial assistance, office equipment etc) over a predetermined period (usually 12 months).

Activity

What experience do you have of drawing up and/or using budgets? If you have, take a few minutes to list the types of budgets, the role you played and the procedures followed.

Continue to work through the chapter and compare the guidelines given with your own experience.

Self-check

How does marginal costing deal with fixed costs?

Answer
Marginal costing does not attempt to allocate fixed costs but treats them as a global sum. The difference between the selling price per unit and variable costs per unit is called contribution. It is a very useful decision-making technique.

Self-check

Here is a marginal costing example for you to work through. Try not to refer to the text.

M & H Wine Producers is a small organisation, making a single type of wine.

Annual fixed costs are estimated to be £36,000.

Variable costs are £1.80 per litre of wine.

The owner estimates that she can sell a litre bottle for £2.40.

Market research shows a potential demand for the product of between 48,000 and 68,000 bottles per year.

Calculate the contribution per unit and the break-even point, and advise whether she should proceed with the project.

Answer
Contribution 60p per litre.

Break-even point 60,000 litres.

The question as to whether the project is viable is a difficult one to answer, and depends largely on the degree of risk the owner is willing to undertake.

60,000 litres per annum have to be sold in order to break-even and this is at the upper level of the demand range. Even at the maximum level of demand the profit would only be £4,800.

Further investigation is required before reaching a final decision, in particular:

— can variable costs be trimmed, thereby giving a higher unit of contribution
— how accurate are the demand figures
— can demand be stimulated by changing the product itself in some way, changing the price etc?

The calculations are straightforward and should have presented no problems. Do not worry if your conclusions differ from those given, since they depend on your assessment of the situation.

Often, budget resource allocations are made by a 'budget committee' consisting of representatives of all major departments. The amounts given to departments are then distributed by further committees within departments. Frequently, budget committees issue both short term budgets, which cannot be altered and long term budgets which can be varied as situations change. Two factors normally determine the period a budget is to cover: the accuracy of currently available information on expected costs, and the degree of environmental uncertainty facing the firm (if the environment is highly unstable the firm will not want to make long-range budgetary plans). Budgeting forces management to think hard about its resource requirements in relation to objectives. Financial discipline is imposed on those responsible for budget administration and increases in cost which cause rapid exhaustion of existing budgets can be isolated and their effects assessed. Spendthrift departments are identified and can be subsequently penalised via reductions in future allocations. Also, the meetings, discussions, joint decision making and general coordination of activities necessitated by budget planning encourage cooperation among departments and the quantitative targets that budgets imply offer a basis for the establishment of departmental and individual objectives.

Budgetary control is an application of the principle of management by exception enabling *periodic* evaluation of expenditure. Excessive costs can be traced back to those responsible, and unacceptably expensive activities can be curtailed. Yet despite its widespread use, budgetary control has many problems, including the following:

- Cost consciousness; essential for effective budgeting, can go too far — causing managers to cut costs by unreasonable amounts. Managers who keep well within their budgets earn the approval of seniors. Hence, some managers regard cutting costs as more important than implementation of the measures necessary to improve performance. Businesses need investment; failure to inject capital obviously cuts costs, but the business might suffer in the longer run.
- To be meaningful, a budget should be broken down into constituent parts, but too much detail in a budget will increase the probability that not all of its components will be achieved since budgets, after all, are *forecasts* of future

spending needs. The more specific the predictions, the higher the likelihood they will be wrong. Moreover, preparation of detailed budgets is time consuming and expensive.

- Some budgets are overspent, others underspent, so that a mechanism is necessary for transferring unused balances to areas which require extra funds. Why then bother establishing detailed budgets?
- Budgets can hide inefficiencies. Once a budget has been allocated the manager in charge may seek to spend the entire amount even though, objectively, not all the funds are needed. Naturally, managers tend to use fully all resources at their command. Wasteful expenditures might occur simply to exhaust outstanding balances.
- It is difficult to distinguish between a budget which has been exceeded because of genuine additional spending needs and one exceeded through administrative incompetence. Indeed, unscrupulous individuals may deliberately overspend in order to have their allocations increased in the next period. Usually, budgets are determined following 'bids' registered by heads of departments in meetings of budget committees. The firm's resources are limited, so not all bids can be met. Heads of department/section realise this and put in exaggerated bids anticipating cuts that will leave the amounts actually allocated roughly equal to their requirements. Budgetary control becomes haphazard in these circumstances.

Budgets may be fixed or flexible. Fixed budgets assume a constant level of activity and resource cost. Flexible budgets relate amounts allocated to appropriate performance indices. Production budgets, for example, are frequently determined by the volume of sales achieved — it is assumed that increasing sales will require additional resources to sustain and continue expansion. Another approach to flexible budgeting is the simultaneous specification of not one but several different budgets for the same department or activity. The budget actually applied will depend on the particular circumstances prevailing at the moment of implementation. Here, the firm recognises the impossibility of foreseeing all future circumstances and so makes allowances for several contingencies.

Allocations of fixed budgets may relate to operations (expected costs are aggregated under various departmental headings and the totals allotted as departmental budgets), or to responsibilities — individuals specify how much they think they will need to attain certain objectives, resources are distributed and they then assume personal responsibility for administering the amounts received. The 'zero-based' approach to budget allocation attempts to solve the problem of managers deliberately overspending in order to increase future allocations. There is no presumption whatsoever that the amount given this budgetary period will be repeated. Indeed, each departmental budget is initially set at zero, assuming thereby that no funds will be made available at all. Hence, heads of department must argue for new allocations at the start of *each* period. Managers are forced to review periodically their plans and working methods and are thus encouraged to identify high-cost activities. The obvious drawback to zero-base budgeting is the enormous amount of time managers must devote to periodic assessments of costs and functions and in repeated presentation of budget demands.

Self-check

List two benefits and two problems with budgets and budgetary control.

Answer

Benefits include comparison of actual outcomes with planned outcomes, yardstick for assessment of performance, ability to trace any variance to its source, makes individuals accountable for their actions, facilitates identification of problems and means of resolving them, forces management to think hard about resources needed to meet objectives, facilitates coordination of activities.

Problems include cost cutting seen as criteria by which management success is gauged, need to utilise whole budget as underspending may result in less funding in the next period, deliberate overspending in order to obtain additional funding in the next period, exaggerated bids for funds in order to ensure that the amount wanted is granted, time consuming.

Installing a budget system

Budgets result from plans which themselves rely on forecasts. Estimates are prepared of the various costs of the activities needed to achieve targets embodied in the firm's corporate plan and budgeted expenditures thus determined for the next accounting period.

The commonest budgeting period is the financial year. Annual budgets will be given to appropriate cost centres (departments for example) which then break them down into budgets for shorter periods (usually months and quarters) and perhaps into budgets for narrowly defined functions — advertising or equipment maintenance for example. The term budget is also applied to certain expectations of outcomes. Thus, we speak of the firm's 'sales budget' when describing planned sales revenues.

Some firms use comparisons of actual and budgeted monthly expenditures to compile 'continuous' budgets whereby the monthly budget for a calendar month one year ahead is based on last month's experience. For example, if February's budget is overspent this year then on 28 February a new and higher budget is set for February next year. This saves the time, cost and inconvenience associated with annual budget meetings, negotiations, forecasting systems etc.

The sales budget is often the first to be established because sales revenues ultimately determine how much the firm can spend. It is not *necessarily* the case that the sales budget is prepared first, although this practice is very common because sales revenues typically represent the 'principal limiting factor' (sometimes called the principal budget factor) which constrains the firm's activities and thus the extent of its spending. However, the limiting factor could just as well be a shortage of labour (in which case a labour utilisation budget will be the first drafted) or a scarcity of raw materials, or restricted machine capacity. In the latter instances the materials or plant utilisation budgets will be the first constructed.

Activity

Which budget is prepared first in your organisation and forms the basis for all other budgets?

It may well be the marketing/sales budget, since most other activities revolve around the marketing plan. While all the departments may be preparing their budgets at the same time, the master budget is likely to be centred on the marketing budget, with all others adjusted accordingly.

The sales budget

This shows anticipated revenues from the sale of target numbers of units of output at certain prices allowing for the effects of bulk order discounts and/or special promotions (money-off coupons etc) and the associated costs of selling output. The budget will be broken down into sales by product and will indicate precisely when various revenues are expected.

All projections of sales income are speculative and subject to considerable error because so many external variables are involved: behaviour of competitors, the effects of advertising, consumer incomes and preferences and several other factors. However, estimates of monthly output requirements are essential for monitoring and controlling production — supplies must be available when and where required, labour needs hiring, machinery has to be acquired, raw materials purchased etc. Marketing and distribution costs depend substantially on sales volume — though not entirely. Thus, salespeople's commissions, travelling expenses and possibly advertising vary with sales volume; while the rent of the sales office, basic salaries of marketing staff and the capital cost of salespeople's cars are largely fixed in value.

The production budget

Production budgets specify the expected costs of creating the output specified in the sales forecast. It needs to allow for the costs of overtime working (perhaps through a separate labour utilisation budget), for warehousing and other inventory costs and for raw materials and finished component purchases. Usually, separate sub-budgets are established for the acquisition of significant inputs. For example, a raw materials budget might be established to plan the purchase and delivery of raw materials and to ensure that storage facilities are available when they arrive. Likewise, a labour utilisation budget could be drafted to itemise the costs of employing and deploying labour. This should include training costs, recruitment expenses and overtime costs and should estimate (normally from past experience) the probable amount of time that will be lost through employee sickness and other sources of absenteeism. Plant utilisation budgets state when and in what circumstances plant and equipment are to be operated, plus their anticipated operating costs (although the capital costs of new equipment are usually dealt with separately in a 'capital expenditure budget' — see below). Maintenance costs may be included here, or placed in a separate overheads budget.

Manufacturing firms which use standard costing might express production budgets in terms of standard labour hours (see above) and material input requirements in standard quantity units. These quantities are multiplied by standard wage rates and materials prices to obtain standard budget cost estimates.

The capital expenditure budget

This defines the new physical resources needed to achieve the firm's production objectives. Some resource acquisitions will benefit the organisation for several years, so capital budgets are usually broken down into sub-units for major and minor projects. Major projects are those which affect the business for many years, even though they may have been paid for in single lump sums. Only a proportion of the capital costs of such assets is set against a particular year's capital budget.

The cash budget

The purposes of cash budgeting are to avoid cash flow deficits while fully utilising cash inflows. Every anticipated receipt and payment must be stated, including allowances for credit sales, bad debts, and for the effects of discounts offered for prompt payment. Missing an important cash flow item can spell disaster for a business — many a profitable firm has collapsed because of sudden and unanticipated cash flow deficits. The expected receipts and payments must be listed strictly according to the month they are likely to occur, regardless of contract dates and details.

Overhead budgets

These may be drafted in categories for production, marketing and administrative overheads. Research and development could reasonably be classified as an overhead and thus included here. Further subdivision is possible into classes for controllable overheads (stationery, cleaning materials and so on) and those which are fixed: rent and insurance for example.

Additional budgets may be prepared for administrative costs such as general management, legal services, audit fees etc and for whichever particular functions (personnel, packaging, distribution, special production processes) are relevant to the firm.

All budgets which are measured in monetary units are drawn together into a *master budget* laid out in a manner analogous to a combined trading and profit and loss account showing (expected) sales revenue less the cost of sales (computed from the production budget) and all anticipated expenses. Capital expenditure requirements are now added, and expected rates of return on expected capital employed worked out. Differences between monthly (say) actual and budget figures must be quickly identified and reported to the managers who are in a position to implement corrective action. It is important that information be transmitted to the people who are empowered to take significant decisions, otherwise much of the effort expended in preparing the budget is wasted.

Activity

You now have an idea of the usual range of budgets prepared by companies. Does your organisation prepare any additional budgets and if so, what purpose do they serve?

Obviously, a range of budgets will be drawn up and possibly amended in the light of discussions, since they are likely to be interdependent.

Budget reports

Reports should be clear, precise and easily understood by recipients. They must highlight problems and, wherever possible, indicate the measures necessary for their solution. The use of standard costing can create difficulties here, because although standard costs, standard labour hours, materials and capacity variances etc have great meaning to accountants and (perhaps) some senior managers they may completely bamboozle the shop floor supervisors who are actually capable of solving problems — provided of course these supervisors fully comprehend the meaning of the budgetary control statements they receive! Simple, straightforward reports are the best. Thus:

- figures should be directly comparable, so that like is compared to like and similar quantities are analysed
- reporting procedures should be periodically reviewed to ensure there is no duplication of information
- information overload must be avoided
- all units and time periods should be clearly stated
- guidelines regarding appropriate remedial action should be available so that a large divergence of actual from budget performance will automatically trigger relevant follow-up action.

Summary

All managers, irrespective of their expertise, need a basic understanding of finance and accounting. Your prior knowledge of this area may have been extensive or non-existent. Should you come into the latter category, this chapter should have given you some insight.

Let us refer back to the annual report you were asked to obtain at the start of the chapter. Study it carefully and try to apply some of the knowledge you have gained. Calculate some of the accounting ratios and see what you can deduce from them.

Note

1 When companies issue shares they rarely demand complete immediate payment. Rather, payment is by instalments, referred to as 'calls' on the company's capital. For example, a share issued at a price of £1 might require payment of 20 pence on application, 10 pence on allotment, a further 20 pence on the first call one month later, 30 pence on the second call two months after that and so on. (Purchasers of shares who fail to pay these calls are liable to forfeit their shares.) The total amount actually paid up on the shares is known as 'paid up share capital', and the difference between this and the share capital actually issued to the public is referred to as 'uncalled' capital. Paid up share capital need not be the same as called up capital because some shareholders may fail to respond to calls. Such outstanding instalments are known as 'calls in arrear'. A

company's 'authorised' (or 'nominal' or 'registered') share capital is the aggregate value of all the shares that its rules permit it to offer for sale. Not all registered capital need be issued. As a matter of record, the value of registered capital will be stated somewhere on the balance sheet document.

8

Managers, the Law and Social Responsibility

Objectives

This chapter will help you to:

- understand the legislation affecting businesses, in particular health and safety, employment, discrimination, unfair dismissal, data protection
- carry out the organisation's statutory obligations as they apply to health and safety, factory acts etc.

Responsibility for implementing a firm's statutory obligations in respect of health and safety, the Factories Acts, fire regulations etc often falls on supervisory managers. Matters arising from the law on unfair dismissal, sex and race discrimination, maternity leave entitlements and so on are typically dealt with jointly by personnel officers and line managers. It is essential that as a supervisor you possess a skeleton knowledge of relevant legal requirements and be able to discuss with others the broad outline of legal issues as they apply to work.

Your position as someone who takes decisions that *may* be in breach of a statute or common law duty is usually (but not always) covered by the doctrine of *vicarious liability* which holds that since you are an employee of an organisation, then your employer is liable for civil (but not criminal) wrongs that you commit in the course of your employment, not you personally.[1] The phrase 'in the course of employment' means acts authorised by the employer or, where they are not formally authorised, where actions are so closely connected with employment that they are *incidental* to the employee's work.

Only if your action is clearly outside the scope of your employment will you be personally liable for your deeds.

Activity

Write down all you currently know about the Health and Safety at Work, etc Act 1974.

As you work through this section, mark off those points you have listed when they appear in the text and make any additions necessary. You should end up with all the salient points for future reference.

The law on health and safety at work

Law on health and safety matters is complex and voluminous. Currently, the most important statute is the Health and Safety at Work, etc Act 1974, which imposes on employers a general duty to ensure so far as is 'reasonably practical' the health and safety at work of all employees. Breach of this duty can lead to a *criminal* (rather than civil) prosecution. Any firm employing more than four workers must, under the Act, prepare a written statement of its policy on health and safety and bring this to the attention of employees. Plant, machinery and other equipment must be safe and well maintained and all arrangements for handling, storing and transporting articles and substances must be safe and free of health hazards. Importantly, your employer is obliged to provide the supervision, instruction and training needed to ensure health and safety. Firms are statutorily obliged to check that all aspects of the workplace are safe, including means of entry and exit, machinery and equipment, and the working environment (fumes, dust etc).

Section 7 of the Act states that employees must take 'reasonable care' to ensure they endanger neither themselves nor others at work. Thus, your staff are legally required to cooperate on health and safety matters, though note that it is *your* responsibility to ensure that instructions are carried out. For example, if protective clothing is necessary then not only must the firm provide it (free of charge) but also you must make sure that it is worn.

The Act is administered through the Health and Safety Commission (HSC) which is a watchdog body that delegates its powers to the national Health and Safety Executive (HSE). The latter issues Codes of Practice which, while not legally binding or enforceable, are looked at by courts when adjudicating cases. Find out whether the HSE has issued a Code of Practice relevant to your industry and if it has, ensure its recommendations are implemented. This demonstrates unequivocally that you are taking 'all reasonable precautions' to ensure health and safety within your department.

The EC Health and Safety Management Directives

A number of important new sets of health and safety at work regulations came into effect in early 1993 in consequence of the UK's implementation of six 1992 EC Directives on health and safety matters. The 1992 regulations on display screen equipment are discussed on page 198. Other regulations in the package are as follows.

(a) Management of Health and Safety at Work Regulations 1992

These require employers to complete risk assessment exercises intended to identify any dangers to the health and safety of their workers or anyone else likely to be affected by the firm's operations. Preventative and protective measures must be specified and a plan for putting them into effect drawn up. Firms with five or more workers have to maintain a permanent record of the risk assessment. The regulations also require employers to establish procedures for dealing with health and safety emergencies and to appoint 'competent people' (who may be outside consultants) to devise and implement the measures necessary to ensure that the firm is complying with health and safety law. Existing UK health and safety legislation is reinforced and extended in the following respects.

- Employees (including temporary workers) must be given clear information about risks, in language they can easily understand.
- Firms must ensure that workers are trained in safety

matters and capable of avoiding risks. Health surveillance mechanisms have to be provided wherever necessary.

- Employees are legally obliged to report dangers and to follow safety instructions.

(b) Provision and Use of Work Equipment Regulations 1992

'Work equipment' is defined under these regulations to include everything from hand tools to complete factories or refineries, while 'use' means *every* aspect of equipment operation, servicing and cleaning. Employers are obliged to make sure that equipment is suitable for its intended purpose and that it is only used in appropriate ways. When selecting equipment, employers must take into account working conditions and the hazards of the workplace. Proper training and information relating to the equipment must be given to workers.

(c) Manual Handling Operations Regulations 1992

These require employers to identify unavoidable handling risks in terms of the size, shape and weight of the load, the handler's posture while performing operations and the ergonomic characteristics of the workplace (space available, humidity, etc). By law, hazardous manual handling operations must be avoided wherever possible.

(d) Workplace (Health, Safety and Welfare) Regulations 1992, and the Personal Protective Equipment at Work Regulations 1992

The purpose of these two sets of regulations is to tidy up and consolidate a large number of existing pieces of legislation currently spread over several different statutes. They concern such matters as the working environment (lighting, ventilation, room space per worker and so on), facilities (toilets, rest areas, drinking water, etc), removal of waste materials, cleaning and maintenance of protective clothing and equipment, and the design and approval of new personal protective equipment.

Safety representatives

If a recognised trade union so wishes it can appoint 'safety representatives' at places of work. The union does not need management's permission for this, but the union must be recognised by the employing firm for the purpose of collective bargaining. Unions themselves decide the procedure for selecting safety representatives, whose functions include:

- investigation of hazards, accidents and dangerous occurrences, and making representations to management on matters arising from these investigations or on any other safety issue
- meeting outside inspectors and receiving information from them
- making formal inspections of the workplace every three months or following accidents or dangerous occurrences
- inspecting and taking copies of any relevant information (accident reports for example) that the employer is statutorily obliged to maintain.

Self-check

Distinguish between the role of the Health and Safety Commission and the Health and Safety Executive.

Answer
The Commission is a watchdog and will advise the Government Minister on any new legislation required or any amendments to existing legislation needed.

The Executive is the operating arm of the Commission and responsible for enforcing the health and safety legislation via its inspectors. The Executive will also give advice to organisations and prepares leaflets etc.

You should positively welcome the appointment of safety representatives in your department and cooperate with them at all times. Active involvement of employees in safety matters helps prevent accidents, acts as a check on the efficiency of the firm's safety records and procedures and generally improves morale. Inspection is an essential part of a representative's duties. Departmental managers are entitled to accompany the representative during inspections, but the Act gives that person the right to confer with his or her union members in private as the inspection proceeds. Notice of an inspection need not be given if an accident or dangerous incident has just occurred.

Following an inspection, the safety representative has to complete a report, one copy of which must be sent to you (as management's representative). The report (books of standard inspection report forms can be purchased from HMSO) will contain a blank section headed 'remedial action or explanation' which you must fill in prior to returning the report to the representative. If you obstruct an inspection or fail to provide necessary information the representative can call in an HSE inspector who possesses legal powers to inspect and this person will disclose to the representative the information you initially withheld. Under the Act, your firm must furnish such 'facilities and assistance' to representatives as they may reasonably require in order to complete inspections. The Act does not specify the meaning of this, although the TUC has issued its own Code of Practice, recommending that safety representatives be provided with:

- use of a room and a desk with facilities for storing correspondence, inspection reports etc
- access to a telephone, typewriter and photocopier
- a noticeboard, and use of the internal mailing system
- access to test equipment and copies of all relevant statutes, regulations, HSE Codes of Practice etc.

If, foolishly, you refuse to make any facilities available at all, the union can bring a case against your firm in an industrial tribunal.

Safety representatives are legally entitled to 'reasonable' time off work on full pay to carry out safety duties and attend union safety training courses. You must be given proper notice of a representative's intention to attend a course, plus details of the course and a copy of the syllabus. Only if the firm offers a comparable course internally may a request for time off be denied.

Safety committees

Should any two safety representatives so require, the firm *must* establish a 'safety committee'. The request has to be in writing and the committee must be set up within three months of the date of the letter. Notes of guidance on the operation of such committees have been issued by the HSC. These recommend that the committee consider welfare matters as well as health and safety, and analyse trends in accidents, diseases etc and investigate specific incidents. It should also develop safety rules and become involved with safety training. According to the HSC notes, the number of management representatives on the committee should not exceed the number of employee representatives, and the management side should be knowledgeable about safety matters and possess 'adequate' executive authority. Note that safety representatives are *not* accountable to the committee, only to union members, and they do not have to obey its commands. Nor does the existence of a safety committee (which might include medical doctors, nurses and other expert members ex officio) imply that safety issues should not be subject to collective bargaining between management and unions.

Many firms employ a specialist safety officer to represent them on safety matters. Full time safety officers (unlike union safety representatives) are not protected against criminal liability if they fail in their duties.

Safety policy

Regardless of statutory and common law duties, you should always pay meticulous attention to health and safety matters within your department. Do not be afraid of being accused of overfastidiousness in these respects; your good example is bound to influence others and hence reduce accidents in the longer term. Accidents are expensive. Not only do they disrupt production, but also they incur the costs of sick pay, investigations, training of temporary replacement workers and so on. Seek consciously to identify hazards and to inculcate in others a respect for safe methods of work. Never authorise or even condone unsafe working practices — try instead to incorporate safety checks into the departmental management *system*. Be seen to investigate all accidents and regularly inspect machinery and equipment. Insist on 'good housekeeping' within the department, and that all accidents (no matter how trivial) be reported. There are government regulations compelling employers to report all serious accidents (and other accidents involving more than three days' absence from work) within seven days and failure to comply with these is a *criminal* offence.[2] The regulations demand that the firm inform its local authority environmental health department *immediately* (normally by telephone) following a death or serious injury arising from an accident, or whenever a *dangerous occurrence* (an overturned crane or a burst pressure vessel for example) takes place. Note that under the regulations, self-employed people and individuals receiving training for employment are covered in exactly the same way as employees. Approved report forms may be purchased from commercial stationers or from HMSO (form F 2508). Records of accidents, dangerous occurrences and outbreaks of certain specified industrial diseases have to be kept for at least three years.

Activity

Take a look at the accident report book for your department/firm and analyse the entries over the past year.

Hopefully, the number of serious accidents will be small, but you may be concerned to see the number of minor accidents due to the same or similar problems.

Accident reports are useful for identifying and preventing the recurrence of dangerous activities. Also, formal records are needed to investigate subsequent claims for compensation from injured employees. Every firm employing more than nine persons, or fewer than nine if the firm is covered by the Factories Act 1961 (see below), is legally obliged to keep an accident book. Reports should be completed as quickly as possible after the incident (before memories fade) and give full details of the victim (age, sex, occupation etc) and of the accident (time, date, circumstances). It should list witnesses, describe the injuries sustained, first aid administered and note whether (and if so when) an ambulance was called and when the ambulance arrived and departed. The cause of the accident should be stated, with details of whether safety rules were followed, whether protective clothing was actually worn, machinery properly guarded etc. When completing an accident report, take a note of what the victim was doing at the precise moment the accident occurred and whether, in the opinion of witnesses, the employee was partly to blame. Copies of the report should be circulated to the worker and his or her union, to safety representatives and to the personnel department. Collectively, accident reports should be analysed to identify recurring causes and the effects of changes in machinery, working methods, pace of production, shift work patterns etc on accident rates.

Encourage your subordinates' interest in safety matters. Watch out for carelessness, tiredness and inadequate knowledge of how to use machines and take action to overcome these problems. Ensure that alleyways are clear, that rough or sharp objects are properly covered, that there is no grease on floors and (obviously) that all machinery is guarded.

External inspections

HSE and other government inspectors visit firms' premises periodically to ensure they comply with various legal requirements. Inspections also occur following complaints by workers or members of the public and after serious accidents. If an inspector finds that an offence has been committed then he or she may inform the employer on the spot of the unsatisfactory item and later ensure that remedial action has been taken; serve an 'improvement notice' compelling positive action within 21 days, or a 'prohibition notice' forcing the firm to cease a risky activity; or prosecute the firm before magistrates. The policy in most cases is to prosecute only if the law is deliberately and persistently flouted. Appeals against improvement or prohibition notices are heard by industrial tribunals. Typically, appeals are based on the grounds that it is 'not reasonably practical' to comply with the notice, eg if the risk of injury was extremely small and the financial cost of complying with the order extremely heavy.

Common sense dictates that you always cooperate with external inspectors. Note too that the doctrine of vicarious liability offers no protection if you do not. Any person who acts in an executive capacity (including supervisors) is personally liable for offences committed under the Health and Safety at Work, etc Act if that person consented to connive with the commission of the offence or if it was attributable to his or her neglect. 'Consent' means agreeing (actively or passively) to the offence; 'connivance' occurs if you become personally involved in committing the offence; 'negligence' means acts or omissions that lead, directly or indirectly, to the offence.

Self-check

What is the significance of an improvement notice and a prohibition notice as served by a Health and Safety Inspector?

Answer
Improvement notice requires that corrective action be taken within 21 days. Prohibition notice requires that an activity perceived as being dangerous be ceased immediately.

Other safety legislation

Although the Health and Safety at Work, etc Act is intended as a piece of umbrella legislation that eventually will incorporate all other health and safety statutes it does not replace existing health and safety laws, which currently operate in parallel with the 1974 Act. The major statutes that you are likely to encounter in your managerial work are outlined below.

The Offices, Shops and Railway Premises Act 1963
This Act applies to offices everywhere, even those on premises normally used for other purposes (factories for example) although temporary offices or those operated for less than 21 hours a week are excluded. Among the Act's major provisions are the requirements that:

- premises, furniture and fittings be kept clean, and that floors be washed weekly
- each person have at least 40 square feet of space
- rooms be properly ventilated, lit and heated (ie to at least 16 degrees Centigrade after the first hour)
- washing facilities with hot water, soap and towels be provided, and that lavatories be accessible and properly maintained
- no worker be expected to lift dangerously heavy weights
- floors, passages and stairs be kept clear and safe, and that all machinery and equipment be guarded
- first aid boxes be provided the contents of which conform to the requirements of the Health and Safety (First Aid) Regulations 1981
- seating must be available, and staff must be given facilities for keeping clothing not worn at work.

The Fire Precautions Act 1971

The essential requirement of this Act is that certain classes of premises (including those covered by the Offices, Shops and Railway Premises Act 1961, factories, and buildings to which the public has access) possess a 'fire certificate' issued by the local fire authority, which must be satisfied that the means of escape from the building and other fire precautions are adequate. Your firm should register its premises with the local fire authority, await an inspection and then adhere to the fire authority's advice. Over and above this, however, you should encourage your subordinates to be fire conscious and to remove fire risks. Ensure that all your staff know how to use fire appliances, the location of fire exits, and how to operate the alarm system. Under the Act, staff *must* be given training in evacuation procedures and the use of firefighting equipment kept on the premises. Moreover, written records of all training sessions must be kept, stating the topics covered during the session, who supervised the session, and who attended.

Inspect appliances and fire exits periodically and keep records of the dates of inspections and the findings. If anyone is sufficiently interested you might consider delegating responsibility for fire prevention to a named person who then presents you with a written quarterly report.

Activity

While the Health and Safety at Work, etc Act covers nearly all work environments, additional legislation exists which is aimed at specific workplaces.

Make sure that you know what additional legislation affects your organisation, and, as with the Act, prepare a brief summary of the main points.

The Factories Act 1961

This contains similar provisions to the Offices, Shops and Railway Premises Act 1963, but for factories. However, additional regulations are included on the maintenance of hoists and lifts and, importantly, it specifies maximum working hours for young persons (restrictions on women's working hours were abolished in 1986) and that all young persons working in factories must be medically examined within two weeks of starting work. A firm may request exemption from the

Act's restrictions on working hours for young persons if it needs to meet exceptional demand for output, provided the firm can demonstrate that adequate welfare facilities will be provided. Exemptions are not issued for more than one year.

Current issues in health and safety

Currently, legislators are not so much concerned with implementing existing legislation, which is mountainous, but rather with dealing properly with entirely new hazards and methods of work.

Visual display units

Perhaps the most problematic new working 'hazard' (if it is in fact a danger) is the effect on workers of protracted exposure to computer visual display units (VDUs). Critics allege that VDU users (especially those who operate wordprocessors) suffer eye strain, headaches, muscular disfunctions and absorb excessive amounts of radiation over long periods of use. It may be that the heat and static electricity generated by VDUs engender lethargy and general feelings of ill health among long term users and this might cause persistent tiredness. Pregnant women and foetuses, it is alleged, are especially vulnerable. Staring into a VDU hour after hour can make workers clumsy, drowsy and unable to think clearly or concentrate. Such accusations are denied by the manufacturers of computer equipment and much research is being undertaken on the subject. The present legal position is that work involving VDUs must conform with the European Community Directive on work with display screen equipment, which is binding on all EU member countries. Under the Directive, employers must:

- analyse display screen workstations to identify potential hazards and take measures to remedy any health and safety problems discovered;
- train employees in the proper use of display screen equipment, inform workers of relevant facts, and consult employee representatives about VDU matters;
- plan VDU operators' daily schedules in order to interrupt long periods of screen work and to create changes of activity;

- ensure that workstations satisfy the technical requirements of the Directive in relation to screen sizes and luminosity, keyboard design, working environment, etc.
- provide employees with eye and eyesight tests prior to their commencing VDU work and at regular intervals thereafter. Firms must supply special spectacles if employees' normal spectacles are not suitable for display screen jobs.

Shift work

Apart from limitations on the ability of young persons to work shifts, there are no legal prohibitions on the extent or nature of shift working (restrictions on women were abolished in 1986). The incidence of shift work is increasing in Britain and with it are the health, safety and welfare problems that shift work entails. These include:

- disruption of biological rhythms (adrenalin secretions, sleep/waking patterns, body temperature etc.)
- reductions in the quantity and quality of sleep, accompanied by constant tiredness
- digestion problems and possible loss of appetite
- disruptions to family life, anxieties about child care, social isolation and worsening social relationships.

Shift workers, on average, have more severe accidents than others and the quality of their output is often lower. There are perhaps two explanations for this. First, there is less continuity of supervision on shift work systems. If you manage each of (say) three shifts for a few weeks or months at a time you will regularly have to supervise a completely new set of subordinates. You establish satisfactory working relationships with one group and then move on to another. Night shift supervision is especially onerous because no administrative support (personnel staff, wages clerks, specialist engineers etc who are at home in bed) is available. Either you must refer problems to day shift managers or take decisions unilaterally without discussing them with colleagues. Second, shift workers are often unable to relax properly, causing fatigue, inattentiveness and accidents. Several weeks are needed to adapt fully to a new time system, but then days off and weekends — when the worker reverts to a normal lifestyle — disrupt the newly established pattern. Ensure that as much preparatory, non-essential and administrative work as possible is done during the daytime. Hopefully, senior management will arrange special transport for workers coming or going at odd hours (when public transport is irregular or unavailable) and provide proper canteen facilities throughout the night. Check that all first aid facilities are available on late shifts and that fire precautions and other safety arrangements are not ignored following dayworkers' departures.

Safety training

Two types of safety training are needed: basic training in rules and procedures and policy training for managers. Basic training can be done via lectures on induction courses. These should include information on hazards in specific jobs, the safety policies of the firm, use of protective clothing and equipment, location and use of fire appliances, first aid facilities, procedures for reporting accidents and evacuation procedures. Further basic training could include first aid courses and regular films/talks on topics such as how to lift weights, identify dangerous situations, attend to injured persons etc. Training sessions should be held regularly and not just when serious accidents have occurred.

Policy training should cover the law on health and safety both generally and specifically in relation to the regulations and Codes of Practice relevant to the industry, plus training on the organisation of safety committees, dealing with safety representatives, inspection requirements, the analysis of statistical data etc. Note that since the Health and Safety at Work, etc Act, s 2 explicitly requires an employer to provide such 'information, training, instruction and supervision' as is necessary to ensure the health and safety of employees, you need from your superiors full details of the legal minimum health and safety requirements applicable to your department's work. Then you can conduct a 'safety audit' to examine checking procedures for equipment and hazardous materials, provisions for storing and handling materials, evacuation systems etc.

Laws on employment

The Employment Protection (Consolidation) Act 1978 is the major statute affecting individual employment matters. It incorporates the Employment Protection Act 1975 which introduced a new series of rights for employees. Under the Act, all employees are entitled to a written contract of employment, to itemised pay statements and to 'guarantee payments', ie up to a maximum of five days' pay (subject to a ceiling amount) in any period of three months for days when an employee is available for work but none is provided.

The Act covers employees who have worked full time continuously for at least two years, or part time but doing more than 16 hours a week for at least two years, or part time but doing at least eight hours a week for at least five years. To be continuous, the employment must not contain gaps caused, say, by the worker leaving the firm and then being re-employed, or by the worker doing less than eight hours a week for a significant period. This and many other aspects of the Act are complex and if you have to interpret such matters you should normally seek advice from your personnel office (which itself may need legal advice). Short term contracts issued one after the other build up continuity in the same way as a single contract for a longer period.

Under the Act, employees have the right not to be unfairly dismissed (see Volume 1 of this series, *Managing People*, chapter 7). Hence they cannot be dismissed for reasons other than gross misconduct, demonstrably inadequate performance, genuine redundancy or some other *substantial* reason. In cases of genuine redundancy, employers must follow a statutory procedure and some financial compensation must be offered. Firms must give adequate warning of intended redundancies and must consult with the recognised union (ie the union they normally deal with) before they are implemented. Firms are required to seek alternative work for those threatened with redundancy and the staff involved are entitled to paid time off to look for other jobs. Criteria used in selecting employees for redundancy must be objective and fair. A worker is 'redundant' when the firm no longer requires work of the type done by the employee. Thus, it is a worker's *job* that is redundant, and not the particular worker.

Redundancy can sometimes be avoided through work-sharing or early retirement schemes. If not, someone must select the workers who are to lose their jobs. Should this unpleasant duty fall to you then you must consider the ages, lengths of service, capabilities, qualifications, experience and past conduct of all the employees who might be involved, taking into account each person's suitability for alternative employment within the firm and you are not allowed to discriminate in terms of race or sex.

Further rules (either embodied within the Act or established by cases heard before industrial tribunals) are listed below.

- workers' representatives must be informed immediately redundancies are proposed. Selection criteria should be disclosed and timetables for layoffs clearly stated
- management should provide reasons for the redundancies and be prepared to negotiate on union proposals for their avoidance. In particular, management should seek alternative work for threatened workers
- before contemplating redundancies, management should stop recruitment, ban overtime, introduce short time working and insist that all employees over normal retirement age retire. Volunteers for redundancy should be sought. As far as possible, the workforce should be cut through natural wastage rather than compulsion
- workers selected for redundancy should be allowed time off with pay to look for other jobs.

Self-check

How would you define redundancy?

Answer
Great care must be taken when making an individual redundant, or a firm risks falling foul of the law.

The word redundancy refers to the work being done and not the individual. Thus if you made someone redundant and subsequently employed a younger, cheaper person to do the same work, this could be construed as unfair dismissal.

Pregnancy and maternity*

An EC Directive on the protection of pregnant workers requires employers to adapt — without loss of pay — a pregnant woman's hours, duties and working conditions, to ensure her

---

* The Government has announced that from October 1994 all women with more than 6 months' service with an employer will receive 90 per cent of their average earnings for 6 weeks, plus statutory maternity pay for the next 12 weeks. Women with less than 6 months' service will receive statutory maternity pay only.

health and safety. Pregnant employees normally engaged on night work have to be given alternative day jobs for a 16-week period, of which 8 weeks must be prior to the expected date of birth of the child. Fourteen weeks' maternity leave are available, with no loss of employment rights (including the right to reinstatement). Two of the weeks have to be taken immediately before the expected date of birth of the child. Pregnant employees are protected against dismissal on the grounds of pregnancy, regardless of their lengths of service. The Directive also requires the protection of pregnant women from specific harmful processes or substances.

Maternity pay must be paid to the woman by the employer. There are two levels of payment: 'higher' and 'lower'. If the woman has worked with the same employer doing more than 16 hours a week for at least 2 years (5 years if she has worked between 8 and 16 hours a week) she can claim from her employer 90 per cent of her normal weekly pay (less the value of state benefit) for 6 weeks, plus the 'lower' rate (set by statute) for up to 12 further weeks. Women with between 6 months' and 2 years' service are entitled to the lower rate for up to 18 weeks. The money is paid by the employing firm, which then reclaims it from the Department of Health and Social Security.

To qualify for statutory maternity pay, the woman must have accumulated 26 weeks' continuous employment by the 'qualifying week', ie, the 15th week prior to a pregnant employee's expected week of confinement. Also, the woman must still be in employment with her previous employer during the qualifying week, although employment for a single day within that week will suffice to meet the condition. Pregnant workers are legally required to give their employers at least 21 days' notice of the dates they intend starting their maternity absences. Notice must be in writing if the employer so requires. If less than 21 days' notice is given, the employer has discretion whether to accept the shorter period and, if the shorter period is not accepted, no statutory maternity pay need be offered. In the latter case, the woman may demand a written statement of the employer's reasons for not accepting the shorter period and may then appeal to the DHSS that it was not reasonably practicable for 21 days' notice to be provided.

It is not possible to fairly dismiss a pregnant woman for being pregnant, even if the pregnancy makes her physically incapable of performing her duties, or if continuing to employ her causes your firm to break the law (there is legislation prohibiting the employment of pregnant women in certain dangerous occupations). In both cases, you must seek suitable alternative work for the woman, on the same pay, and if none is available you must 'suspend' her on full pay for the appropriate period. All pregnant women are legally entitled to paid time off to attend 'reasonable' numbers of ante-natal appointments. However, firms are entitled to ask to see letters confirming that female employees are actually pregnant and that appointments have in fact been made. Note that you cannot fairly dismiss a woman for reasons 'connected' with pregnancy. Thus, dismissals of women suffering from emotional tension brought on by pregnancy, or suffering from post-natal depression, or who miscarried and were consequently ill, are unlawful.

Following the birth of the child, the employee is legally entitled to return to work in her old or an equivalent job. The woman must give notice of her intention to return. This notice must be in writing and submitted at least 21 days before taking maternity leave. If the employer writes to the employee within 7 weeks of her confinement, asking for confirmation of her intention to return to work, she must reply within 14 days. A woman who has completed 2 years' continuous full-time service or service of more than 16 hours a week, or five years if she has worked between 8 and 16 hours a week, is legally entitled to resume work any time up to 29 weeks after the birth (with a possible 4-week extension on medical grounds), provided she gives at least 21 days' notice of the date of her return.

To qualify for the right to reinstatement, the woman needs to have been continuously employed for at least 2 years immediately prior to the 11th week before the expected date of confinement (or 5 years if she worked between 8 and 16 hours a week).

Other rights under the Employment Protection (Consolidation) Act

Other important rights conferred by the Act are the right to a minimum period of notice of dismissal (one week for each year of continuous service up to maximum of 12) and, for employees with more than 2 year's full-time service (5 years for part-timers working more than 16 hours per week), the right to a written statement of reasons for dismissal and the right of employees to take time off work for public duties such as serving as a justice of the peace, local councillor, school governor or as member of a regional health authority.

Discrimination

The Sex Discrimination Act 1975 aims to eliminate discrimination between men, women and married persons. Under the Act, it is generally unlawful for an employer to discriminate on sex or marriage grounds in recruitment, in the terms and conditions of employment offered, or in the provision of access to training or promotion opportunities. 'Direct' discrimination occurs through treating people less favourably on account of their sex or because they are married. 'Indirect' discrimination means imposing a condition such that the proportion of members of one sex who can meet the condition is considerably less than the other, eg a statement in a job advertisement that all applicants must be over six feet tall. 'Victimisation' results from people being less favourably treated because they complain of not receiving their statutory rights, or because they help someone else complain of unfair treatment.

There are exceptions to the Act, notably:

- employment mainly outside Great Britain
- employment in religious organisations that operate a sex bar
- certain occupations where Parliament has decided women should not be employed
- employment in the armed services.

Also exempt are jobs where sex is a 'genuine occupational qualification'. Examples are actors who play male or female roles, jobs in single sex schools, hospitals or other institutions and jobs where 'decency or privacy' require employment of a particular sex (lavatory attendants for instance).

The Race Relations Act 1976 offers similar rights to ethnic minorities. As with the Sex Discrimination Act there are several exemptions, including work where membership of a particular race is a genuine occupational qualification[3]. Responsibility for seeking to eliminate racial discrimination in employment lies with the Commission for Racial Equality, which publishes Codes of Practice to guide firms in these respects. Similarly, the Equal Opportunities Commission issues Codes of Practice in relation to the avoidance of sex discrimination. Both Commissions conduct research and initiate legal action against firms that unlawfully discriminate.

Industrial tribunals

Workers who believe they have been unfairly dismissed under the EPCA, or subjected to sexual or racial discrimination, or who wish to register complaints under a variety of other employment regulations and statutes (including health and safety and equal pay legislation) may initiate actions in industrial tribunals. These are independent courts consisting of three persons: two lay members (one from each side of industry — employers' organisations and trade unions) plus a legally qualified chair-person. Procedure in tribunals is meant to be informal relative to other courts (members wear ordinary clothes, not wigs and gowns). Nevertheless, a body of case law has arisen around statutes (such as the EPCA) interpreted by tribunals, precedents have been established and much legal jargon unfamiliar to the lay person is used. This is particularly noticeable where one party to a dispute is represented by a solicitor or barrister (or both) while the other is not.

A case begins when a complainant (referred to as the 'applicant') completes form IT1 (called an 'originating application') which he or she obtains from a Post Office, job centre Citizen's Advice Bureau or the DHSS. The form is easy to complete and requires only brief particulars of the applicant and the alleged offence. IT1 is then sent to the local office of the industrial tribunal (the address is provided with the form) where it is photocopied. One copy is sent to ACAS (see Volume 1 of this series, *Managing People*, Chapter 10) and another to the employer (called the 'respondent') who must complete and return form IT3. The latter is known as a 'notice of appearance', and is sent to the employer with the copy of the originating application. Again, form IT3 requires only brief details of the employer's defence. Copies of the completed IT3 are sent to the applicant and to ACAS. An officer of ACAS then attempts to settle the matter out of court. He or she will offer to visit the complainant at home to discuss the case and will offer to speak to the employer. ACAS officers act only as intermediaries and are not allowed to take sides. If no out of court settlement occurs a date is then fixed for the tribunal.

Having seen an outline of the other party's case, either side may request 'further and better' particulars of its substance. For example, if an employer states that a worker who alleges that he or she was unfairly dismissed was actually sacked for incompetence, the worker may demand precise details of the supposed incompetence. An employee accused of being persistently late can ask for the dates of his or her supposed latecoming. If a party refuses to supply further particulars, the other side can ask the tribunal to order their provision. Refusal to obey such an order results in that party not being allowed to present a case when the tribunal convenes. This means that only one side of the story is heard so, normally, the party presenting the case will win. Similarly, both sides may request copies of documents that are relevant to the proceedings, eg contracts of employment, internal memoranda concerning disciplinary action, letters to outside persons (excluding legal advisers), work rotas, and so on. As with 'further particulars', a party can apply for a tribunal order that such documents be produced, with similar consequences if the order is not obeyed. Copies of all the documents to which either party intends to refer during the hearing must be sent to the other side a 'reasonable' time before the hearing takes place. Usually, the tribunal itself will want to receive copies of relevant documents prior to the hearing. Witnesses can be called to give evidence (on oath) and may be subpoenaed by the tribunal if they are reluctant to attend.

If there is doubt about the tribunal's ability to hear the case (if, for instance, the employer alleges the complainant has not completed the necessary amount of continuous employment to claim unfair dismissal) then a 'preliminary hearing' may be called at which the tribunal will investigate its powers to hear the case. Also, if having quickly examined the superficial facts of the situation the tribunal feels that one party's case is certain to fail — say because a dismissal was obviously unfair, or because a disgruntled worker has initiated a case frivolously or vexatiously simply to annoy the employer knowing full well that it cannot succeed — then a 'pre-hearing assessment' will be convened to establish agreed facts and, if appropriate, warn one of the parties that its case will probably fail. If the party receiving the warning wishes to proceed with the case, it may do so (before a different tribunal, so that the eventual outcome is not prejudiced) but will be required to pay a £150 deposit and may if it loses be ordered to pay the costs. Normally, each side must bear its own costs, and tribunals are extremely reluctant to award costs to one of the parties even if the other party has been warned of this possibility at a pre-hearing assessment.

Self-check

What action can the tribunal take if it feels, based on the information submitted to date, that one side cannot win?

Answer

The tribunal can make its feelings known and warn the party concerned that its case will probably fail. However, that party has the right to choose to proceed with the case under a different tribunal.

Usually the employer (or the employer's representative) speaks first at a tribunal hearing, though in sex and race discrimination cases the applicant normally begins. A brief opening statement is presented, witnesses are called and are examined, cross-examined by the other party and then questioned by members of the tribunal. Then the other side makes an opening statement and calls witnesses and then both sides sum up. The tribunal may alter the order of proceedings to suit particular circumstances. At the end, the tribunal privately considers its decision which is announced either on the spot or, if complex legal issues are involved, within a couple of days. Reasons for the decision are later confirmed in writing. Appeals are allowed and are heard first by the Employment Appeals Tribunal and then by higher courts.

Appearing before a tribunal

As a manager, your likeliest personal contact with an industrial tribunal will be as a witness on your employer's side. In this case, you will enter the room where the tribunal is to be held as one of the several members of your firm's party and sit just behind the person who is to present the employer's case. The three members of the tribunal sit facing the court behind a long table on a dais about a foot higher than the rest of the room. On being called you sit behind a table at right angles to the court, swear to tell the truth and are then questioned in turn by your firm's representative, the other side and by members of the tribunal. You must recount events, give dates and times, confirm the existence of documents etc. An important difference between an industrial tribunal and other courts is that hearsay evidence can be allowed in a tribunal. Also, you can be asked leading questions and may be allowed to read a prepared statement on a complex point. All parties sit while speaking.

Many cases, especially those where only limited evidence is available, are won or lost on the standard of presentation of witnesses. If you are in the right and tell the facts honestly without omission or embellishment, you should make a powerful impact. Speak slowly (the tribunal members will be taking notes by hand), clearly and take care not to repeat your points. Mention only relevant matters, do not be sarcastic or aggressive. In particular, do not make unpleasant remarks about the complainant — project yourself as an agreeable, reasonable and objective person. You should, of course, be well dressed, clean and tidy.

Documents are the best means of proving a case and the more comprehensive your records the better. Thus, in a dismissal case for example you should have copies of carefully worded written warnings, memoranda to the personnel and other departments, written evidence of your having actively tried to avoid the dismissal (say through offering extra training, a change of department, detoxification help for an alcoholic etc) and of your being *reasonable* at all times. If a worker was sacked for bad timekeeping, you need written evidence (time cards for instance) of all the times he or she was late. The firm's representative will lead you through your evidence. You will then be cross-examined by the other side, which will challenge your version of events and seek contradictions in your evidence. When challenged, reply slowly — take your time and if your mind goes blank simply pause, take a drink of water and politely ask for the question to be repeated. Then, repeat the question in your own words, ie you say, 'So the question is . . .'. By this time your mental capacity to deal with the matter should have returned. The chairperson of the tribunal should ensure that you can give your evidence without being harassed or bullied, though you must answer all relevant questions. Be sure you *fully* understand the applicant's complaint and why that person feels so aggrieved that he or she is prepared to go through the harrowing experience of an industrial tribunal. Assume that the other side will ask the questions you least want to answer and check that you have sufficient information to deal with them. Points deserving special attention include the following:

- did you possess the formal authority to do whatever you did (eg dismiss the worker) and did you have written evidence of this authority at the time the action was taken?
- were all provisions of relevant Codes of Practice strictly followed? If not, why not?
- is any crucial evidence missing? Do you have all the documents necessary to support your statements?

The better prepared you are and the more logically you present your material the more impressive your evidence will appear. Do not express opinions about the meaning of laws on particular issues. This is the role of the tribunal and the representatives of the contesting parties. Be prepared, however, to explain company documents and procedures. While doing this bear in mind that internal administrative systems mean little to outsiders, so avoid technical jargon and ensure before the hearing that you can describe, simply yet comprehensively, any company-specific procedure that you might need to refer to when giving your evidence.

Activity

Having read through 'Appearing before a tribunal' carefully, you will now realise that the watchword is preparation. You must have all the documentary evidence and be sure of your facts before giving your evidence. You are not there to give opinions but to describe events.

Miscellaneous legislation

There are other laws and statutes which you should know exist, but need not know about in detail. For example, the Employers' Liability (Defective Equipment) Act 1969, provides that when a worker is injured because of a defect in the equipment provided by his or her employer and the defect is the fault of a third party (the equipment's manufacturer for instance) then the injury is deemed to be also attributable to the negligence of the employer even if no actual negligence has occurred. The employer can of course sue the third party for any loss suffered.

Under the Employers' Liability (Compulsory Insurance Act) 1969, every employer must insure against liability for bodily injury or disease sustained by employees in the course of their work and a copy of the insurance certificate must be displayed on the premises.

Another important piece of legislation is the Occupiers' Liability Acts 1957 and 1984 which require the occupier of premises to take 'such care as in all the circumstances is reasonable to see that visitors will be reasonably safe in using the premises for the purpose for which they are invited by the occupier to be there'. Visitors are defined as persons on the premises for the benefit of the occupier (customers for example), guests and those entering under contract. Note that under the Unfair Contract Terms Act 1977, notices warning of dangers or hazards will not necessarily relieve an occupier from liability for injury to visitors — notices proclaiming that, 'Persons entering these premises to do at their own risk' have no legal effect.

Social responsibility

Progressive businesses are increasingly concerned to be 'good' employers and neighbours. Being a good employer and neighbour means implementing equal opportunities programmes, showing concern for the environment and for consumers, operating fair and impartial grievance and disciplinary procedures, paying fair wages and offering security of tenure to employees. A good employer, moreover, will design jobs to secure maximum job satisfaction in employees and will encourage their participation in management decisions that affect their working lives. As a good neighbour, the firm will avoid polluting the environment, will settle its bills promptly, have concern for the quality of its output and not engage in unfair competition. Many organisations today publish formal statements of their intention to behave equitably. They print long equal opportunity statements at the ends of job advertisements and issue to employees all sorts of declarations regarding training, staff development and promotion policies.

Activity

This exercise requires you to research a straightforward statute, the Offices, Shops and Railway Premises Act (OSRPA), and apply the statute to a set of complaints. You will find a copy of the OSRPA in the main library in your area.

You have been approached with a number of complaints by the staff representatives for your section. They are as follows:

1. A few months ago there was an outbreak of graffiti in the building and certain offensive words were daubed on an office wall. No attempt has been made to remove or paint over the graffiti.
2. Female employees (who are in the minority in your department) have to go to another department (where the majority of workers are female) in order to visit the lavatory as there is no females' toilet near to your section.
3. There are 220 people in the building but only one first aid box.
4. The first aid box is seven minutes walk away from your section.
5. Three workers share a small office with:
   (a) 120 feet of floor space, and
   (b) a ceiling 9 feet high.
6. An office junior is expected to operate a shredding machine which she feels is dangerous; and she is not sure how to operate the machine.
7. No drinking water is available in the department or in nearby toilets.
8. The office windows have not been cleaned for seven weeks.
9. The office overlooks factory premises and the air coming through open windows is sometimes very dusty.
10. One of the machines on the factory premises that the office overlooks is extremely noisy and causes unpleasant vibrations.
11. A pregnant woman is required to operate a word-processor with a VDU for four and a quarter hours a day.

Refer to the OSRPA and address the following points for each complaint:

- find out whether it is covered by the Act — if it is not, you should say so.
- state the precise legal position, specifying the relevant sections and paragraphs of the Act.
- write out the legal position for each point, quoting the relevant section and paragraph numbers of the Act.

Activity

Take a look at a recent job advertisement published by your organisation. Does it make any statement regarding equal opportunities?

In your opinion, does the statement reflect practice, or is it merely lip service to the legislation?

Too often, however, organisations pay only lip service to their proclaimed social responsibility objectives. Some firms have equal opportunity policies yet continue to employ the great majority of women in lower grades and do not even consider ethnic minority candidates for advertised positions, internal candidates' applications for promotion are not properly assessed and there is much use of casual labour etc.

Why then do such firms bother to issue equal opportunity statements? There are, perhaps, two (equally cynical) reasons. Internally, a much publicised equal opportunities policy offers glimmers of hope to currently disadvantaged groups and it placates trade union and other worker representatives, particularly if the latter are comfortably positioned and looking for excuses to justify not helping their less fortunate colleagues. Externally, the existence of formal policies appeases outside bodies, governments, shareholders, agencies and Commissions (the Commission for Racial Equality, for example) that press for implementation of good employment practices. Provided the organisation is *seen* to be making token gestures such bodies will not interfere in its internal affairs.

In reality, equal opportunities and other socially responsible policies are doomed to failure unless the managers who operate them are personally committed to these ideas. How can you help promote good employment practices, especially equal opportunities programmes, within your firm? Your first task is to *identify* problems. Look critically at the situation in your department in each of the following areas.

Female workers

Are the numbers of men and women roughly equal at all grades within the department? If not, why not? If you are male, you

Activity

Take a look at the people who work in your department and their grades. For each grade, count the numbers under the following categories:
Male: White
          Ethnic minority
Female: White
          Ethnic minority

The higher the grade, the fewer females and members of ethnic minorities you are likely to find.

How do you account for this, when there is legislation prohibiting discrimination?

should recognise that older women, who have taken time out for child rearing duties, are just as valuable to the firm and have exactly the same capacities for acquiring skills and useful work experiences as their younger male colleagues. Encourage female staff to attend courses and to apply for promotion. If the personnel department offers (as it should) career counselling for women, urge female subordinates to attend. You may be able to organise work schedules, responsibilities and functions in order to allow female staff greater flexibility in their working hours, especially during school holidays and to enable women to gear their work around the school day.

Male supervisors should not participate in sexist conversations among male colleagues or share sexist jokes; they should make it known that they will deal sympathetically with women subordinates' complaints of sexual harassment via grievance and/or disciplinary procedures.

Disabled people

Much unfair discrimination against the disabled is unintentional and caused by ignorance rather than animosity. Never assume that a disabled person is not capable of doing a job without first discussing the matter with the person concerned. Try wherever possible to adapt working methods, facilities or equipment to accommodate the needs of disabled employees.

Ethnic minorities

Racism at work results in the undervaluation of the contributions of ethnic minority employees. 'Positive action' is sometimes advocated as a means for promoting the interests of ethnic minority groups. Positive action is *not* the same as positive *discrimination*, which itself is unfair. Rather, positive action means measures whereby people from minority groups are either encouraged to apply for jobs in areas where they are under-represented or are given special help and training to enable them to develop their skills and abilities in order to compete effectively for certain kinds of job. Such assistance can raise the expectations of ethnic minority workers, encourage loyalty to the firm and motivate these employees to greater effort.

Indices of the effectiveness of an equal opportunities policy include the number of complaints registered by minority group employees, changes over time in their average wage or salary levels, the ratios of applications for jobs or promotion to selection of candidates from minority groups, the incidence of training activities among minority workers and the reasons they give for resigning.

Dealing with racism

Managers may experience the effects of racism either through complaints received from ethnic minority subordinates or through a racist (or sexist) atmosphere created by unpleasant remarks, racist 'jokes', unofficial segregation of racial groups and covert discriminatory practices. You have, in my view, a moral as well as a legal obligation to try to prevent race (and sex) discrimination. It is important to establish a working environment in which all, and not just some, employees feel valued, comfortable and emotionally secure. Note immediately the difficulties created here by the (still) common practice in many firms of employing women or certain ethnic groups to do particular types of low paid and/or casual or part time work. Not only does this affect adversely the minorities involved, but also it encourages more favoured employees — usually white males on higher pay and secure full time contracts of employment — to view these minorities with contempt, simply because they are seen to occupy low status positions.

Activity

Have you ever encountered racism in your department and, if so, how did you deal with it?

Racist acts can vary from unpleasant remarks and jokes to physical violence and intimidation. The threat of disciplinary action may stop some practices, but the only long term solution is to change attitudes.

The author suggests that you obtain copies of the relevant Codes of Practice and ensure that you do not encourage racism and discrimination through your actions.

Answer the questions posed in the text as you work through it. You may be surprised at some of your findings.

Some organisations now incorporate anti-discrimination clauses into their disciplinary codes, with explicit provision for the suspension, and ultimately the dismissal, of staff who engage in discriminatory behaviour. Without doubt, formal rules can prevent some discriminatory practices, but they do not necessarily change *attitudes* towards various racial groups. Rules against racially or sexually abusive language are especially useful, since abuse of this nature inhibits minority group employees from participating enthusiastically in work-groups and encourages non-acceptance of minorities by the existing staff.

Obtain copies of the CRE and EOC Codes of Practice and make sure your department follows their recommendations. Critically examine your induction courses and procedures to ensure that all new entrants are made *equally* welcome regardless of race, sex or indeed any other distinguishing characteristic (physical disability for example). How many ethnic minority workers are employed in less attractive jobs? Do they receive on average lower pay than other employees and if so, why? How many of your direct and immediate subordinates — the ones with whom you share confidences and jointly take decisions — are from ethnic minorities?

Ask yourself honestly whether you expect different standards from minority group employees. How do their qualifications compare with the level of work they undertake? Are your ethnic minority subordinates less inclined to discuss their work with you, or to approach you with problems and, if so, why?

State legislation or internal company rules cannot, of

themselves, remove prejudice at its source. More important is quick and effective replacement of biased opinions, perceptions and values among existing employees with completely new outlooks. Norms of prejudice and discrimination must be replaced by attitudes consistent with equal opportunity working practices and, as a manager, you have an important role to play in these respects; ritualistic specification of what *ought* to happen in equal opportunity programmes will not lead necessarily to genuine non-discriminatory behaviour. Threats of transfer, demotion, suspension or the sack may temporarily suppress outward manifestations of sex, race or other discrimination, but the prejudice that causes these problems remains; indeed, it might actually worsen through being repressed. Violently hostile emotions towards minority group employees might then persist indefinitely.

Attitudes that unfavourably predispose existing employees towards minority groups are easily formed and difficult to eradicate. Typically, workers are completely unaware of the wider contexts in which minority group recruits are brought into the firm. Confronted for the first time with non-conventional entrants they might respond only to the minority recruits' ethnic, sexual, or physical disability characteristics, not seeing their (perhaps formidable) personal strengths and technical abilities and these responses will relate, of course, to stereotyped perceptions of the minority groups involved. Training is obviously important here and the EOC and CRE Codes of Practice lay great emphasis on this. Try therefore to incorporate material on equal opportunities into your departmental induction programme and any other non-technical training courses for which you are responsible.

Breaking discriminatory habits is difficult, particularly when (as is usually the case) people do not recognise the existence of their prejudiced views. Do not patronise existing staff, but make it quite clear that you do not approve of race or sex discrimination. If subordinates and other colleagues react negatively to your promotion of equal opportunities, ask them to suggest alternative strategies that will keep the firm within the law: a few minutes' rational reflection on the implications of continuing (illegal) discriminatory working practices is normally sufficient to convince people of the need for change.

Perhaps the most effective way of dealing with a prejudiced individual is to put that person to work directly alongside minority group employees. Biased people who are forced to *depend* on members of an unfavourably regarded group are made to compromise their prejudiced behaviour.

Activity

Have you tried the method of dealing with a prejudiced individual outlined in the text?

Perhaps you might like to try it out the next time you come across the problem and assess its effectiveness for yourself.

Remember always that if you are accused of practising racial or sexual discrimination you may have to defend your actions before an industrial tribunal. You must be able to demonstrate that unlawful discrimination did not take place and that at no time did you intend to discriminate unlawfully. Thus, none of the documents you issue — letters, memoranda, notices, instructions etc — must even imply that members of a particular race or sex will be unfavourably treated. This is especially important for correspondence relating to recruitment, training, promotion, selection for redundancy or other forms of dismissal. Retain copies of all documents received and issued in these connections, and inspect them regularly for evidence of bias, real or implied, or unfair discrimination.

Summary

This final chapter has dealt with many complex and contentious issues, but no one said that the manager's role was an easy one.

As a front line manager, you must have a working knowledge of the legislation that applies to the working environment, and this is by no means an easy task as legislation is constantly being amended, superseded etc.

Notes

1 Common law is law that has evolved over centuries from decisions given by judges on cases brought before them. Statutory law is enacted by Parliament. It creates new rights and obligations but, in interpreting a statute, common law concepts must often be applied.

2 Reporting of Injuries, etc Regulations (1985), SI 1985 No 2023. Similar provisions apply under the Factories Act.

3 The exceptions are:

- employment in a private household (although victimisation remains unlawful)
- employment outside Great Britain
- employment of seamen recruited outside Great Britain (Asian sailors, for example, may be paid lower wages)
- discrimination authorised by Parliament (racially discriminatory immigration laws for instance)
- genuine occupational qualifications.

Index

Other titles in the Effective Supervisory Management Series

Managing People

Preface

1 **Recruitment, Selection and Induction**
   Objectives — Recruitment — Selection methods — The problems involved — Employment interviewing — Induction — The exit (termination) interview

2 **Training**
   Objectives — Evaluation — Training methods — Techniques of training — Computer based training — Group training — National Vocational Qualifications (NVQs) — Management training

3 **Performance Appraisal**
   Objectives — Performance reviews — Critical incidents — Potential reviews — Reward reviews — Appraisal interviews — Usefulness of transactional analysis — Equal opportunities considerations — Further problems with performance appraisal — Legal aspects — The EOC Code of Practice

4 **Counselling**
   Objectives — What counselling is — Counselling methods — Directive versus non-directive counselling — The counselling interview — Is counselling really worthwhile?

5 **Job Evaluation**
   Objectives — Why have job evaluation? — Devising a scheme — Problems with job evaluation — Legal considerations — Measuring equal value through analytical job evaluation — Jobs that are not equal

6 **Handling Grievances**
   Objectives — The need for formal procedures — The case for informality — A model grievance procedure — Causes of grievances — Dealing with grievances

7 **Dismissal Procedures**
   Objectives — The role of the individual manager — Legal constraints — Employees with AIDS — The disciplinary procedure — Action short of dismissal — Absenteeism — Other Codes of Practice — Taking disciplinary action

Personal Effectiveness